Bards Against Hunger

10th Anniversary Edition

Edited by
James P. Wagner (Ishwa)

Bards Against Hunger

Copyright © 2023 by Local Gems Press

www.localgemspoetrypress.com

Bards Against Hunger

www.bardsagainsthunger.com

For Every Poet Who Used Their Words To Make A Difference…

Foreword

Bards Against Hunger was founded in 2013 by the Bards Initiative, a poetry group on Long Island, NY that hosts many readings and publishes local anthologies. The leaders of this group came up with the idea to host a poetry reading that would gather food for the hungry around Thanksgiving time as a way for poets to give back to their local community. The poets of Long Island loved the idea and flocked to help organize, read at the event, and gather food.

The event was such a success that the group decided to make it an annual event--and keep the tradition strong and growing each year. Then, the sister-group NoVA Bards in Northern Virginia decided to do the same thing in solidarity and raise food for the local pantries in their area. Then, poetry groups in other states started to join in the cause one after another and there were events in Pennsylvania, Connecticut, Wisconsin, Indiana, Kansas, Texas, California, Maryland and Delaware, North and South Carolina, Florida and more.

To date there have been almost 100 Bards Against Hunger readings across the country. And we aim to continue the tradition for many years to come.

This 10 year anthology is a celebration of a lot of the poetry that has been shared in the spirit of giving, and is comprised of 200 poets from around the world.

The proceeds from the sale of this anthology will go to helping Bards Against Hunger grow, and host more events to raise more food for local pantries and food banks.

Table of Contents

UNITED STATES

NEW YORK

Sharon Anderson

Among the Fallen

When I was small
I danced among the leaves
weaving in spirals
of unchecked joy
chasing a dream

When I was young
I gathered fallen leaves
tossed them aloft
in a spin of delight
feeding a dream

As I grew old
I sprawled among the leaves
feeling them wither
along my spine
leaching my dreams

And now as I repine
I hold a single leaf
follow the veined design
and ache to know
if ever it held a dream

Sharon Anderson has been published in many international and local anthologies, has been nominated for a Pushcart prize, and has six publications of her own poetry. She serves on the advisory boards of the Nassau County Poet Laureate Society,co-hosts readings at Oceanside Library, and hosts the PPA poetry workshop at Farmingdale Library.

Mark Blickley

Buzzed

It takes 100,000 buzzing vomits
to create one pound of honey
inside my head

Our moisture will evaporate
as my nectar
converts into your honey

A foraged energy source of
sweet offerings you ingest
to thicken into honey

Creating within me
the cells that seal
my honeycomb

for later consumption.

Mark Blickley grew up within walking distance of New York's Bronx Zoo. He is a proud member of the Dramatists Guild and PEN American Center. His latest book is the flash fiction collection *Hunger Pains* (Buttonhook Press).

v.j.calone

Waiting on Superman

Does he even know that he's my father,
and that he had himself a son?
Some say you were bruised or mentally used
by the man of mystery and myth.
When asked, you said, "He's probably dead
or out there hunting in the woods."
But, you're confused an utter recluse.
Alone and in need of talking off the roof.

I just want the truth,
just gimme some truth,
because, I'm not waiting on Superman.

Does he even know you gave me up?
That he could've had himself a pup?
Did you ever give him the unannounced news?
You see, as I follow the clues, the numbers calculate,
but, still don't add up. It's a zero sum game,
which was ended early by rain,
and pours out the hole left in my heart.

But, I still have to fill the cup,
and I don't intend to sound abrupt,
but, I'm not waiting on Superman.

Did you even care for me? Do you? You must.
People say you celebrate my birthday every year.

6

I think that's sweet, but rather odd
when I am only a phone call away.
But you live in a well, a thick plated cell,
an impenetrable fortress of doom.
So I wait and I write of how I still feel.
But, I'm okay with where I am today.

Cause I know we will find a way.
Lord, please help me find a way,
and we're not waiting on Superman.

Jamie Ann Colangelo

Childhood Memories

Many memories of childhood
some were sweet and some not
the times we had out east
at the summer country house
with family filling the kitchen
and pancakes filling our bellies

The long barefoot walks on asphalt
tarring the kitchen floor, mama yelling,
trips to the lumber yard, waiting in a hot car,
visiting the only general store
with the best ice cream sandwiches

Day trips to Smithpoint Park
echoing voices in the tunnel
horseback riding and ice cream eating
these and many more are some of the sweetest,
most memorable times of my childhood

Susan Collender

Imagine a world without hunger or war
All diseases now have a cure
Cooperation and brotherhood
Striving for the greater good
A world of friendship and peace
Where hatred, violence cease
Focus on helping and caring
A world where we would be sharing
We all wish this would be the case
Where all people would embrace
If only we could create this ideality
If only we could all make it our reality

Susan Collender is from Long Beach, NY. She had a career as a guidance counselor and has two children and five grandchildren. She has been published in *Trees in a Garden of Ashes: Poetry of Resilience*, *UFT Reflections, UFT Musings*, the *Long Beach Herald*, and many other publications.

Paula Curci

I'm Sorry

I was angry and I told him so.
I lit a candle and let it flow.
I hollered and howled.
Snarled and growled.
I'm sorry, I got an attitude.
Sorry, I don't have gratitude.
But when I saw that girl in the hallway there-
I knew she carried deep despair.
I tried to talk to her, tried to share
but she couldn't see the
gift you gave me.
I just don't understand.
She refused to shake my hand.
My head was spinning.
No one was winning.
Questions were floating.
The devil was gloating.
Confusing my faith, with my with fear.
Rousing my doubts right here.
If love is what she was looking for?
Why didn't she knock at your door?
Or why didn't you answer ... further more?
Conflict was beating my soul,
Why for one is it Flowers, and the other Coal?
Dismayed, I shook my head.
Only to hear a celestial voice that said:
"Your harvest has been granted,

because of the love you have planted.
You are forgiven.
Steer clear of what is forbidden.
Explain the things that have been hidden.
Reflect upon the Passion play.
Try to find a place to pray.
and you will come to know-
although,
pain has filled your day …
… I too, have felt this way."

Paula Curci is the Nassau County Poet Laureate (2022-2024). She hosts Calliope's Corner: The Place Where Poets and Songwriters Meet and What's the Buzz ® on Radio Hofstra University. She is the co-founder of The Acoustic Poets Network ™. Curci has developed a style of recitation called Posics™, a combination of poetry and singing. Her work can be found on streaming services, Kindle and in various anthologies. Curci has won a Nassau County School Counselor of the Year, a national Gracie, and several LI Press Club awards. She has received a Citation from the City of Long Beach, NY, for her dedication to poetry and cultural arts. Curci resides in Long Beach, NY.

Margaret Curtis

The House of Imagination

I grew to be a woman
In the house
Of Imagination

It was empty so I peopled it
With characters
From the books I knew

Henry Thoreau was my brother
Mark Twain was my good friend
Justice Oliver Wendell Holmes was my just father

I lacked for nothing

Margaret Curtis (Cuda), PhD earned her doctorate at Lehigh University. She lived in Pennsylvania and taught there for twenty years; it was her second home. Nevertheless, she was born in Olean, NY, and now lives in Dunkirk, NY, one mile from Lake Erie.

Joan Dobbie

My Father In Heaven On Yom Kippur

My Father has lived in Heaven
for what seems like eternity

On earth
he was a good man
He gave food to the hungry

In Heaven
he is a good man still
But he has no food to give

In Heaven there is no time
There only *is*
It is always now

And now, in Heaven
Yom Kippur *is*

My Father is a good man

Because it is Yom Kippur
he enters the synagogue of Heaven

He is fasting. It seems
he has been fasting forever
Nor does he take even one drop of water
to ease his thirst

My Father feels the gnawing of hunger
in his belly—the rasping in his throat
the pounding in his head

There is thunder,
There is fire
The heavens are howling

In Heaven there is no time
Yom Kippur in Heaven
is now

The Heavenly congregation is
huge — innumerable— the men,

in the men's section
draped in their heavenly blue and white
prayer shawls

their heads, covered against the pain
of their hunger

their deep pain-filled voices chanting in unison
they rock and bow and moan

We have sinned
We have sinned
We have sinned

With clenched fists
they are pounding their hearts

They are praying to the tune
of the hunger of the world
They pray for the end of hunger

They pray for the life of the one
who is starving
—of the masses —- innumerable—
who are starving

whose bellies are bloated
whose skins thin as paper
whose eyes, still living, are growing dim

My Father is feeling the pain
of their starving
The Heavens resound with the pain
of their hunger

Until they are fed
the sun will not set
on Yom Kippur
in Heaven

Joan Dobbie, daughter of Holocaust refugees, was born in Switzerland in 1946 and raised in rural Northern New York. Theirs was the only Jewish family in town. Her father, the only doctor for over 40 years, is to this day remembered for what a good, caring, person he was. Joan now lives in Eugene, Oregon, where she co-hosts the Windfall Reading Series and is (by default) the new President of her local Literary Guild.<joandobbie.blogspot.com>. She has a 1988 MFA in Creative Writing from the U of O. Her latest chapbook, Zenyatta/Joanna, Finishing Line Press, came out in April, 2023.

Kathaleen Donnelly

Flowers

In their infinite realm of design,
that which brings us to awe
each time we open our eyes—

take a breath, clear the mind
of all else, just be
in the moment, like a reprieve
from the everything,

let the vision be the all,
colors, patterns, contours,
their flow, reach, natural place

to live, thrive, grow, flourish—
is to bring us to a certain knowing,
what perfection is given to us,
gifts, like the body.

Our imaginations want to reproduce
them in our own voice, within our own
skills, bring the natural to works of art.

Another form of perfection from the
same minds that see, need to take the
transient to the permanent, share with
everyone without access.

Are we designed to appreciate
beauty? It's all around us,
 impossible to ignore.

Flowers would grow even if not attended,
despite us all; soil and rain, sun, shade,
finding a place in the world to be
their natural selves

allowing us to enjoy, maybe,
not picking for short term adornment.
How does it feel to be picked?

What do flowers sense? Do they warn
others to find homes amongst the rocks,
under tree branches or old browned
leaves left over the seasons?

Do they let weeds deter us, their inferior
selves, let them take the hit? No matter,
they too, have their own perfection.

Kathaleen Donnelly is a 1976 graduate of St.Vincent's which was in Green-
wich Village, who currently works at SBMC as a Nurse Practitioner in Car-
diology. With a little help from her friends, she produced *Paumanok, Poems
and Pictures of Long Island, Interwoven and Transition*. She loves the written
word, strives to write something you'd like to hear.

Patricia (Rispoli) Edick

Aging Without Grace

My voice is weak
That's what I see
Not strong like it used to be
My mind wonders
Like a ship lost at sea
My body no longer limber
My bones are weary
 My knees are weak
I am a stranger to myself
This can't be me
My friends are the same
An older version of themselves is what I see
I don't like it here
But where can I go
When I lay down my head
Dreams come to me
The People and the places I see is where I long to be

Patricia (Rispoli) Edick is from Long Island, New York and is a retired Civil Servant. She is of Italian Descent. Patricia is a published author of short stories and poetry. This is her second poem for Bards Initiative Books. She is the Author of a Children's book. Patricia is a member of The Long Island Writer's Guild.

Adam D. Fisher

It Is Raining

It is raining. Not the fine rain
of a summer shower but big
drops, the kind that hit the pond
and make a splash, then a ring
that goes out and out,
the kind that hits rose leaves
and makes them bounce, the kind
that hitting an empty tin can
lets out a constant plunk, plunk,
the kind that soaks sheets
left on the line to dry in the sun
before someone can come out
to take them down. The kind that
passes quickly, making way
for the sun.

Adam D. Fisher is the author of poetry, stories and liturgy including four books of poetry: *Rooms, Airy Rooms* (Writers Ink, Cross Cultural Communications and Behrman House), *Dancing Alone* (Birnham Wood/ LI Quarterly), *Enough to Stop the Heart* (Writers Ink) and *Hanging Out With God* (Writers Ink.) He was Poetry Editor (2006-2014) of the CCAR Journal, the Journal of the Central Conference of American Rabbis.

Florence Gatto

Sustenance

They await the plane landing
The New Delhi air Is heavy with steamy heat
They anrticipate a gift of sustenance
The passengers deplane holding a gift
The hungry eyes with growling stomachs on slender limbs
Graciously accept the containers of airplane service meals
Each traveler donates to out stretched hands of famished souls
Namaste they say
As others hurry to their luxury hotels

Born in Brooklyn but considers herself an Italophile. She studied in Perugia
Italy with a Fulbright grant She celebrates Her ancestry in her memoir "The
Scent of Jasmine(pub Legas) Vignettes from a Sicilian Heritage. She writes a
coumn for The Golden Lion Order Sons and daughters in America newspa-
per .Florence facilitates workshops for the L.I.Writers Guild.

G. Gordon

Blind Faith

In faith
I step out
 in faith
 today
I breathe
in faith
 I believe the sun will rise
in faith
 I believe the moon will not fall
so men and women can land on it
in faith
 I believe the Messiah will return
in faith
 I believe for a better world
in faith
 I believe
 the truth will set us free
one day
in faith

G. Gordon's photography, poetry and short stories are inspired by her faith in God. Her work has been exhibited at the Creations Art Shows at OSA in NYC. She Attended John J. College. Gordon resides in the state of New York.

Daryel Groom

Orange Moon

I wait upon an orange moon
green eyes, black hair
a witches broom
sounds of ghouls
birds of flight
black bats a fright
hallows eve close at hand
spooks and scares
terrifying tales
bumps in the night
and old haunted places
spirits ghosts and all frightening faces
black cats, mirrors, ladders
spiders, cobwebs in shadowy spaces
coffins, vampires
monsters of the dark
howling werewolves
dancing skeletons shaking the cemetery at dark
reveling beneath an orange moon

Daryel Groom has had numerous poems and short stories published in college literary magazines such as Nassau Community College *This is Big Paper* and Molloy College's *Curiouser Curiouser*. Additionally, she has had the following poems published *"Phantoms"* in the 2019 edition of Nassau County *Voices in Verse* and *" Archangel of Peace"* in *Bards Annual* 2020 edition ,*"The Summer Town"* in *Nassau County Voices* in Verse 2022, *"I Teach the Kids That"* in *The Nassau County Voices in Verse* 2022, and *"Ode to My Aging Feline Friend"* in *The Friendship Anthology* on Amazon edited by Sourav Sarkar 2022. Furthermore, she contributed to an online grant publication entitled *"My American Ancestry"*. Most recently her poem entitled *"The Summer Town"* featured at The Long Island Fair hosted at Old Bethpage Restoration September2022. She resides in Long Beach, New York.

Sheila Hoffenberg

Changing Seasons

Sitting in front of the campfire, roasting marshmallows
The sun has faded away
Singing songs to get us in the mood
A cool breeze blows through our hair
Crackling sounds as the lights flicker
The burnt smell of toasty marshmallows
The stars are looking down on us
The moon appearing in the sky
A beautiful night of wondrous thoughts
Relaxing, calm, lost in the moment
Now once again I am sitting by the fire
There's a chill in the air
I wrap myself with a cozy warm blanket
For now the summer has left us
No more sitting outside by the fire
Watching the flames dancing in the fireplace
Telling us that winter has arrived

Sheila Hoffenberg has been published in a POETRY ANTHOLOGY 1983, the PPA 2016, 2019, 2021, 2022 and 2023,NCPLS 2018, 2019,and 2023. BARDS, PRINCESS RONKONKOMA 2019 and Suffolk Poetry Review 2020. A featured reader at the Levittown Library and Sip This 2019 and Honorary Mention at the LI Fair 2022 and a member of the LIWG since 2012.

Maria Iliou

If I Only Knew Then

Revisiting past
If I only knew then
My younger self
Is autistic

I hear you on that note
If only I can go
Back in time
Visualizing sceneries

My mind replays
Replaying in room of
My brain

Remembering intensely
Focused on film
Moments…memories
Teary eyes…sorrow

Smiles emerges
Emotions
Deeply within
Bubbles bursting

Autistic giggles of laughter

Would things have
Been different
If I only knew

Q. Imagine

Raindrops On Windows

These raindrops on windows
haven't felt the essence of breath.

The cold touch of a windy night
that's led to a loveless death.

As the air fills with misty steam
for moments
we haven't felt it yet.

And I sway into your touch
and burn
for a love to feel,
if I let.

This guard of coated armor
fall away from the scorn
and the pain.

To allow these woes
I hold and simply fall
and lose the strain.

I hide these stains.

These scars that drain
the love

until it rains.

I yearn to feel ecstasy
if euphoria can find a way.

This coated armor
that's held in fear
needs to fall away.

For I, to bask
and feel that deep sensation
of a love
to take.

As I sway into your touch
to find
a love I dare
to make.

I close my eyes
and give way.

To the woes and fears
of yesterday.

For the night
holds something true.

I gaze at the windows,
and you.

Q. Imagine is an author with two books on Amazon. She is a screenwriter and poet, who published over 500 poems and short stories on the internet. She has been featured in a poetry collection titled, The Embrace Of Dawn as well as in Libretto magazine. Other than writing, she is an avid lover of nature, gardening, exercise and food.

Nurit Israeli

Bouncing Back

My gorgeous orchid, the purplish beauty,
died unpredictably. Or so I presumed
when her flowers wilted
and her petals curled down,
failing to thrive.

Orchids can be fastidious –
succumbing too soon if not treated just so.
But I wasn't ready to release
my previously vibrant flower.
Not yet.

Caretaking is complicated.
Overwatering may overwhelm.
So I kept her soil just moderately moist,
fed her neither more nor less than needed,
and moved her, to shield her from wind,

and, would you believe it?
My limp orchid perked up,
stretching upright,
flaunting a burst of brand new
pristine purplish petals.

Yes, sometimes what seems final isn't:
Just the correct quantity of water,
good enough food, the right light,

a tender touch, a hope.
Nothing more...

Dr. Nurit Israeli holds a doctorate in psychology from Columbia University, where she was associate professor of psychology. Nurit is an award-winning poet published in numerous international poetry anthologies, *The New York Times*, *Writer's Digest*, and other online and print magazines.

Alma Johnson

Where do I go from here?

It had been a long lengthy travel
The road has been rough…. The years went by fast.
Been very committed. COMMITTED to the purpose. Made this commitment
MY priority.
Many sacrifices made. You would never even believe if told.
Working times two with Pride and dignity. Kept up with Responsibilities.
Many times, the escape was to participate in Positive actions.
Organized in all aspects of life. Tried to fit in to find something to do where
success could be appreciated. Experienced a push back, rejection, left alone.
Despised.
Success was not to be questioned. All help is from the Lord.
Jealousy came around uninvited which then lead to should I call it HATE.
Hence there is not a place of acceptance. Even when performance is Right,
Enjoyed, praised, done with excellency still there is not a Place, No acceptance. NO Embrace.
Searching searching…. Been to many places…. It ends up being the same.
One last effort to work with the burden given for a SPECIFIC place. Attached
to the individuals involved.
Performed well, then, can you guess what happened?
Rejected again.
Where do I go from HERE????????

Ryan Jones

Ideological Sustenance

You can plow, you can sow
You can tend, you can reap
You can thresh, you can chaff
You can work yourselves to the bone
We never do such things

You can tame, you can breed
You can raise, you can groom
You can feed, you can ward
You can supply your livestock's needs
We never do such tasks

You can grind, you can stock
You can store, you can save
You can dry, you can salt
You can prepare for the hard times
We never plan for that

You make it, you feel it
You see it, you smell it
You hold it, you have it
You just cannot taste or eat it
Only we can do that

You labor, not savor
You exert, not retire
You hunger, not consume

You no longer sustain yourselves
Only we deserve that

You wither, we strengthen
You grovel, we impose
You resist, we murder
You are but skin, callus, and bone
Only we will survive

You lose it, we force it
You hide it, we find it
You need it, we eat it
You are under starvation's clock
We are now your hard times

Ryan began writing at an early age and believes it to be the best way to express one's thoughts and ideas. Ryan's topics of interest include nature, human and natural history, mythology, and personal and collective experience, all of which are influential to his writings. Ryan holds a bachelor's degree in English with a master's degree in childhood education, and has worked with children by profession.

Daniel Kerr

Taking My Brother To Church

My brother Jeff battled alcoholism and depression;
whenever these dark forces got the better of him,
I suggested he find a church.
It will bring you closer to God, I said;
the scriptures and sacraments will aide you in your battle with booze;
and the church community will support you.

"Where was God when I lost my right eye," Jeff would respond.
"Where was he when my first wife died from cosmetic surgery?"
"Where was he when my second wife dies of a brain tumor?"
He was hanging on a cross, I said,
sacrificing his life for us,
and waiting to hold you in his loving arms.

No matter how many times I took him to detox,
or visited him in hospitals and rebab centers after his latest fall,
I could never get him to church.
"If God exists," he said,
"I'll meet him on the water,
he can find me on Long Island Sound."

As I planned Jeff's funeral over the phone,
the priest asked if we had body or cremains.
I have his ashes, Father.
"Do you have an urn?"
When I said I had his ashes in a tackle box,
the phone line went silent.

I think he looked for God on the water,
and this was what his daughter requested.
"Then let us respect his daughter's wishes," the priest responded.
The Entrance hymn was *We Shall Gather at the River*,
And the Offertory hymn was *Eternal Father Strong to Save*,
otherwise known as the Navy Song, made famous by the Titanic movies.

As the bagpipes played *Amazing Grace* at the end of the funeral mass,
and I carried his ashes up the aisle,
it hit me that I finally got Jeff to church.

As I watched his daughters spread his ashes on the water,
I knew Jeff would meet God on Long Island Sound.

Daniel Basil Kerr, CPA, Ph.D. is a cross-cultural consultant focused on help-ing people and organizations be more inclusive and work more effectively across borders. He teaches accounting at St. Joseph's College and Suffolk Community College. Dan is the moderator of the monthly All Souls Church *Second Saturdays* poetry reading. His poems about religion, politics, history, and "growing up in Asharoken in the 1960s" have been published in *Bards Annual, Suffolk County Poetry Review, Performance Poets Associa-tion, Beat Generation*, and other anthologies.

Mindy Kronenberg

Sunday

Thirteenth Avenue in Borough Park
came alive in the morning
as my father and I walked the rows of stores
for our Sunday morning feast, a sepia memory
in filtered light as I leapt at each window
to his approving laughter, our bundles growing
with baked goods, cheeses, meats,
and flowers for our table.
There she is-- the small girl skipping along
the many Brooklyn blocks, her hand in his.
There he is-- as he whistled and kept
his boisterous stride, walking back
to the awakened building, walking up
to the tiny kitchen, walking through
the doorway lit by
the delight in my mother's eyes.

Mindy Kronenberg is a widely published poet, writer, and professor of writing and the arts at SUNY Empire State University. Her work has appeared in hundreds of print and online journals around the world, in numerous anthologies and video recordings, and has been featured in art exhibits at galleries and museum installations. She is the author of *Dismantling the Playground,* a poetry chapbook, *Images of America: Miller Place*, a pictorial history, and an illustrated book of poems, *Open*. She has recently appeared in LTV's *The Pianist, The Poet, and The Painter* performance, a live/televised fundraiser for the arts.

Thomas Aquinas Landers

ABBONDANZA!

I've been slow to own God's generosity.
Now that grace finally opened me a crack,
I've learned Her abundance is reality.

Mom imbued a sense of scarcity and lack.
Fear and anger said there was never enough.
Grab for it or give up. The future is black.

If there is not enough, I must puff and bluff.
Being not enough informed my constant fear.
Hiding my low self-esteem made living rough.

Terrified of anyone getting too near,
Feeling less than always required an escape.
These escapes inevitably made life drear.

There was never ever enough of the grape
To hide me from myself and my behavior.
Would I find rest under the funeral crepe?

But then Amazing Grace became my savior.
A professor teaching me "Human Freedom"
Was "the light unto my path" to freedom's door.

I received love and acceptance and then some.
I was showered with these until I believed.
Soon I was joyfully singing "Te Deum".

In knowing I was enough there came relief.
I was loved until I developed self-love
And rid myself of the limiting beliefs.

Embracing the truth I was worthy of love
Allowed me finally to risk trust in God,
A God Who's keeping for me a treasure trove.

Experiencing abundance is not odd,
But that it took me so long to see the truth.
I'm blessed to see the gifts wherever I trod.

I don't have to be a celebrated sleuth
To now know God loves me and She will provide.
Abandoning myself to God makes life smooth.

While joyfully living in veracity
I've been slow to own God's generosity.

Thomas Aquinas Landers is a social worker living in Oceanside, NY with his fabulous wife, LInda. Thomas, a life long lover of poetry, was challenged by a friend in 2020 to write poetry. He has been at it ever since and is loving it.

Billy Lamont

coins in a paper cup

a democracy
is a bureaucracy
when those in authority
don't represent the majority

the subways stink of piss
and the homeless lie lifeless
trash can clothes
grocery cart closet
alleyway bedroom

a recession
is a depression
when the workingman with the blue collar
sweats blood for an extra dollar
and still can't feed and clothe his family
in a hopeless economy

a recession
is a depression
when trying to get ahead
is like running in a revolving door
like someone once said,
"the rich get rich
and the poor just stay poor"

politicians practicing nepotism
as they tell me, "don't fight the system"
a system where you need money to succeed
a system that promotes corporate greed
a system that overlooks the people who are in need!

a democracy
is a bureaucracy
when those in authority
don't represent the majority

Billy Lamont is a multimedia poetry performer who has performed on national television a number of times, including MTV and Joe Franklin Show, toured and performed with rock festivals such as Lollapalooza, and appeared on major radio stations across the U.S. He has three books of poetry and nine album CD/digital download releases. His latest book *Words Ripped From A Soul Still Bleeding: Poems For The Future Edition* is available at Barnes And Noble and Amazon as a paperback, or as an eBook, and all his albums can be streamed on Spotify and Apple Music.

Patricia Leonard

She Lives

I remember the crashing waves at her feet as she spun me around the summer of '93. The sun kissed pillows of her lips perched sweet memories. Honey eyes and long black hair glistened with salt water and sand as if she was a mermaid touched on land. Her toffee skin blemish free rubbed smoothly into me as I exited her womb 23 years ago. Coconut oil and white diamonds rush through my nostrils faster than bread fresh out the oven on a Sunday morning.

She died twice on the table while I signed a lease to an apartment across the country, her husband by my side. A little biventricular robot was installed in-between arguments of who had the rights to say how we would continue the path of life or death. Blue birds sang in the background of my busy mind while the crows circled the future carcass. She thought it was the flu and went to sleep, as many women do. She was no more than 52.

Patricia Leonard is a 35 year old poet, short story and creative non fiction writer born and raised in New York. She has her BA in English linguistics from CUNY York College and her MFA in creative writing at CUNY City College of New York. Her work has been featured in Three Rooms Press' yearly anthology, Maintenant 10, 11, 12, 13, 14, 15, 16, and 17. She has also been featured in The Voices project, Broke Bohemian, Hamilton Stone, Culture Cult, Fleas On the Dog and for a second time in The Bards against Hunger anthologies.

Melissa Longo

Mind's Eye

Awake now;
And I forget my dreams that came before me;
the brain has these tendencies

I wander late and lonely; lusting for connections necessary for the heart

Wonderland
How do I transverse to this place
A beast is in my minds eye

Awake now;
And I forget my dreams that came before me; the Brain has these tendencies

Wonderland
I'm coming for you
A beast is in my minds eye

Spiraling downward; down down down
Obligations have transitioned from persuasion probing; proving that we must
remember

A beast is in my minds eye
And it's coming for you here in
This land of wandering
The visions are erratic sans prophetic

Awake now;

And I forget my dreams that came before me; the brain has these tendencies;
Spiraling as we go down down down

Gaining power in the threshold
The beast was within me
Wandering through my mind as faeries do in the forest; preying upon those
whom wronged them; changing in front of our own eyes

These ones awaken
Transversing as we spiral
Destroying

Melissa T. Longo: a New Yorker, poetess and kalimba player. Sometimes she is a comedian in between her pieces. Melissa is now learning how to be an IT Technician or Computer - whichever comes first. She hopes that you enjoy her poems and have a bountiful harvest.

Debbie De Louise

A Typical Teen

She's 15
my only child
my daughter, a teen
She was born early but ready for the world
She can be angry but never mean

She stays up late
hours after dawn
snacks at midnight
chats hours on her phone

Her room is a mess
no place to walk
She can be quiet
but loves to talk

She uses Essential Oils
lights candles
and in magic dabbles
We don't fight, but we have our squabbles

She's bright, an animal lover
especially cats
she's sensitive to her weight
and thinks she's fat

She's pretty and sweet

a whiz at PC's
Her drawings are quality art
She's always late
but finishes what she starts

She'd like to grow up to be
an anime artist, cook, or nurse.
maybe all three
She's environmentally aware
drinks coffee but prefers tea

I love her more each year
even when she makes me scream
My daughter is perfect
a typical teen.

Debbie De Louise is a retired librarian and the author of the Cobble Cove and Buttercup Bend cozy mystery series. She's also published five standalone novels and a collection of cat poems. Her stories and poetry appear in dozens of anthologies, including the Red Penguin Collection, the Bards Annual, and the Nassau County Voices in Verse. Debbie lives on Long Island with her family and two cats. Learn more about her and her work at: https://debbiedelouise.com/about/

Sheri Lynn

V-day February 2001
written on Valentine's Day February 14, 2022

*"Each time a woman stands up for herself,
without knowing it possibly, without claiming it,
she stands up for all women."* – Maya Angelou

I arrived alone
sat in a front corner of my stadium section
with a clear view of one magnificent woman after the other
gracing the stage, sharing vulnerable feats of courage
amidst Vagina Monologue performances at The Garden

was it Oprah or Jane Fonda or Gloria Steinman or…
who asked the New York City audience
"When a question resonates with a violent act
you experienced anytime in your life, please stand.
Please remain standing through all questions."

The first question did not apply to me
and I sent heart whispers to all who stood there
the second question set siren screams in my ears

stand

breathing stopped as I pushed up on armrests
stood, holding decades of jailed pain

I realized I was the only one standing

48

in my entire section
no other section looked like mine
their near eyes on me caused a fainting blush
body trembles, sight fell to black
from where it came – this fortitude will
it did not let me fall or fail or sit
quiet tears dripped onto my hands gripping
the railing in front of me
sight evolved to a blur, to a keen gaze
at the teenage girl on stage
with a net over her eyes
beneath a bodied burka
who shared of her harrowing escape
from the Taliban…

I must
stand

upon my return home holding a
red ribbon each of us were given and
asked to wrap around trees—
with trembling arms and hands, I tied myself
in solidarity to people like me

together we stand
"to end violence against girls and women"

16 years later
"me too"

I am
Standing

Sheri Lynn, was published by: *Ms. Magazine, Chicken Soup for the Soul: Listen to Your Dreams, Long Island Quarterly, The Long-Islander: Walt's Corner, Paumanok Transitions* (also a co-editor), *Nassau County Poet Laureate Society, , Bards, Performance Poet Association, Nassau County Voices in Verse, The North Sea Poetry Scene Press, 911 Memorial Museum, Poets4Haiti* and more. Sheri Lynn launched BreatheInsights.com with her first poetry/photography chapbook *Nature's Breath* published by Dream Believe Publish in 2019; was a Long Island Writer's Guild & Long Island Author's Group member before moving to Virginia in 2023.

Joan Magiet

From The 747

The day hangs below.
It stretches across white-capped Rockies.
Patches of brown terrain surround
desolate ponds, tired palm trees
warmed by a gentle zephyr.
It cradles the plane
that brings me to Palm Springs.

Mist presses at the window.
It obscures my reading light.
I think into clouds that join
in a crescendo as we fly.
My neck and shoulders relax
like the unfastened seatbelt.

The borders of my life
 expand like sunshine.

Joan Magiet is the author of two books of poetry, Tender Chains, a collection
of poems written from the heart and Haiku for Jewtalian Mothers, a collection
of humorous haiku which will make you smile as you recall fond memories.
She is a former Assistant Professor of English, SUNY, Nassau, adjunct fac-
ulty and an award winning journalist and poet.

Joe Maldonado

I walked the beach and thought

A poem is a glittering stone in the sand
You pick it up and
 the sun hits you square in the eye
A sniff brings hints of sea salt and ancient life
It's solid
 and soft
 and rough
at the same time
You know you can't eat it
 yet it fills you up
Then it leaves you with the question
Do you bring it home and stick it on a shelf
Or do you throw it to the ocean
 for others to find,
to hold,
to feel

Joe Maldonado is a poet from New York. His work can be found in numerous anthologies and the collections *Subterranean Summer* and *Skeleton American.*

Gene McParland

Soup de Jour

It's a good thing that I don't spend my time
counting my losses,
because I'd need a calculator,
which I don't have.

To count my gains however,
I don't even need to take my shoes off
to tally that count.

My life has been one of
too many black cats crossing my path;
too many manufacturing companies
torn down to build shopping malls.

No pension. No gold watch.
but plenty of overdue bills
still coming to my address.

Forget about the Top 1%,
I'm fighting to stay out of the bottom 5%.
You realize after a while that no one
wants your resume,
or what you have to offer,
so you struggle with what you have.

Not much to be happy about it seems,
but hey,

I don't have to worry about break-ins;
there's nothing to steal.

Besides it always fun
to check out the soup de jour
while standing on line
down at the community soup kitchen!

Gene McParland (North Babylon, NY): is a graduate from Queens College and possesses graduate degrees from other institutions. He has always had a passion for poetry and the messages it can convey. His works have appeared in numerous poetry publications. He is also the author of <u>Baby Boomer Ramblings</u>, a collection of essays and poetry, and <u>Adult Without, Child Within,</u> a collection on poetry celebrating the child within. In addition, he also acts in local theater and in videos, and has written several plays.

Rita Monte

Above the Clouds

search
wonder
create possibilities
jump on the moon
dance in space
feel the
crescendo of your heart
rise
soar
embrace the lunar energy
listen to...
 the sublime songs
of the stars
the sun
the planets
enjoy every step
every rhythm
every journey
traverse
transform
discover a new earth...

above the clouds

CR Montoya

Hopeful Eyes

I've seen the wide eyes of a child
who just received a desired gift
a smile so broad it lights the room
brings laughter to the gift giver
and shared joy for all participants.

I've seen the sad expectant eyes
of a child when mom comes home
without milk, bread, and without hope.
The desperation of a parent
who doesn't know where to turn
who fears foremost for their child.

I've seen the eyes of the food pantry volunteer
when a donor brings, "just what's needed."
Simple things, soup, coffee, pasta,
dry goods, and the occasional child's snack.

Thank you, the volunteer exclaims.
I know just where these will go
there's a family down the road
where the breadwinner is out of work
they're trying, praying for guidance.
This food is an answer
a small miracle, and a response to prayer.

I've felt the joy of knowing I've helped.
If just a little, others will benefit,
I wish I could do more,
the thought families struggling -- hurts.

I'll keep doing my part
in hopes of seeing bright, smiling eyes,
in hopes that we're doing better.

Together we can succeed.
Together, we can win.
No matter where you live
the need is great all over.
Let's work together
let's do all we can.

Hunger can occur anywhere,
eyes fade to sorrow.

Strive for smiling eyes,
together, we can do it.
Care about your neighbor,
care for others less fortunate.
Every contribution helps.
The blessings you'll receive -- Priceless.

CR Montoya publishes children's stories, featuring *Papa The Happy Snowman*. He published a short story titled *Return to Bedford Falls* in January 2022. Based on the movie *It's A Wonderful Life*, the story carries readers through time describing how the lives of the movies glorious characters evolved after that fateful Christmas Eve. All his stories can be found on Amazon.

George Northrup

Grand Theft

She had left her guitar on the stage,
and as the audience filed past
security guards at the exits,
I wanted to seize the instrument
and disappear with it backstage,
from there into the night.

I might be noticed.
I might be asked,
"Where are you going with that guitar?"
Nonchalantly I could answer,
"Rosa asked me to fetch it for her."
Maybe that would work, maybe not.

I could find myself talking to police,
cuffed to a felony that wrecked my career.
But if the theft transformed the hopeful thief,
I would feel myself nestled beneath her breast.
I would feel the tips of her fingers on my fret.
I would be plucked into her song.

George H. Northrup is a poet and psychologist in New Hyde Park, NY. He is the author of *You Might Fall In* (2014), *Wave into Wave, Light into Light: Poems and Places* (2019), *When Sunset Weeps: Homage to Emily Dickinson* (2020), and *Old Caterpillar* (2021).

Angela M. Parisi

An Angel For Me

Sometimes I hear a whisper, or a touch like it's the wind.
I know she's right beside me, this is how it all begins.

I wake up every morning with a smile upon my face.
Joyfully the day begins, for I know I'm full of grace.

Her presence is always with me, even though she isn't seen.
My friends they laugh and tell me it's just a foolish dream.

My heart begs to differ, for I know angels are real.
And my angel does protect me, it is the real deal.

And when at night I go to bed so peacefully I sleep,
My angel watches over me, she never makes a peep.

I know she's right beside me, I sense her like the wind.
When dawn arises in the morning, this is how it all begins.

Angela is a graduate from Queens College, NY with a BA in education and social science. She has self published two books "DD and JuJu" and "DD and JuJu Welcome Della". She also had her short story "To Grandmother's House" published in the Scribes Valley 20th Anthology and poem "Bullying" in LI edition of Newsday. Angelas loves music, writing and gardening.

Sherri London Pastolove

Don't Fall for It

it was there
mixed in with the
heavy late-summer humidity
the wisp of a breeze
an early autumn breeze
and then like fairy dust
poof - gone
it surfaced again in tv ads
hawking pumpkin
flavored everything
in woolen clothing
weighing down mannequins
in college football
watched with sandy beach toes
the relentless push of
the calendar
seasonal hopscotch
hop forward
skip the last blissful
glowing rays of summer
only to wistfully look back
shivering in an early
November snow

Sherri London Pastolove has published two poetry collections, *Cowgirls* and *Love in D Major*. Her poems have appeared in *Ms. Magazine, Newsday, NCPLS Reviews (Honorable Mention 2022), October Hill Magazine,* the *911 Memorial Artists Registry, Corona: An Anthology of Poems, Long Island Quarterly and The Bards Annual 2021.* You can follow her blog @ www.sherridarling.blogspot.com.

Diana Poulos-Lutz

What is Freedom?

Do we rejoice or mourn,
as Fredrick Douglass declared?
For liberty and independence
for all must truly mean for all
who are in this land,
male, female, all shades of
human, all the tall and short,
whether accounts of wealth
or struggle in city or country,
all the ways we love
or dress or walk down a street--
how does the sparkle in that fire-
work shine light on freedom
in every corner and hall of
our great land?
Who do we look down or up at
and when we look inside
do we see others as truly worthy
in the same degree as one another?
May the rainbow display above rise up
and raise up the sentiment of man,
that tomorrow the independence
of all is not just but a dream, but
the way we live, love and breathe
equity, free and brave
so that we may rejoice for more
than that for which we mourn.

Diana Poulos-Lutz is an award-winning poet from Long Island, NY. She has a B.A., M.A., in Political Science from Long Island University, as well as an M.Phil, Master of Philosophy in Politics, from the New School for Social Research. Diana's poems have been featured on various media sites, performed at various locations, published in local anthologies and her books, Time to Rise and I Walk On, are available on Amazon. Diana's poetry is inspired by her deep connection to the natural world, along with her desire to promote equality, mindfulness, and empowerment.

Kelly Powell

Drawing from Life

There is a hunger in the glaring light of the 24 hour
Walgreens on Route 25 in Selden . A hunger that only
appears as the night creeps her way toward midnight.
A hunger for working a second shift or for milk for
morning coffee, for earning a little extra money
for Christmas for two young children or for endless
rice and beans or ramen, comfort food lacking
nutrition but sustenance just the same. Lacking
a spiritual connection, based only in the the sensations
of this earthly plane and all its faults. A spiritual
connection to the cashier whose form appears
to turn toward the harsh, glaring light and back
and forth and in and out of shadows contouring
her achy, overworked figure. The spiritual connection
to the harried, the hurried, the listless and the sublime
shining and shining like angels of the workaday
world chiming 12 times on their car keys, the change
in their pockets and electronic payments. The bright
eyed millennial hides in plain sight, tapping on
her phone like a patron saint of boredom in the blind
spot she has come to know in the cross hairs where
the boss and the security cameras won't see her.
Behind the seasonal aisle decked out in its best
back-to-school ensemble, marble composition
notebooks, nestled with the giant binders covered
in logos and squishmellows and primary colors,
loud reds and yellows and blues next to Halloween

bric a brac. The horizon line divides the infinite
snack aisle from the over-the-counter medications
and health and beauty aids, calamine to jalapeño
kettle chips racing to the vanishing point of cold
drinks and multitudes of angry bottled water
competing for space next to the expired milk.
How is it that her form is turning through space?
When will she emerge from the shadows to help me
find my photos ordered online two weeks prior
and left behind because of the endless rushing
and rushing and rushing of day to day existence.
Two different shoes on, ready for the boardroom,
to volunteer at the pta bake sale, and onto the wake
of a childhood friend's gregarious father lying in state
or a classmate who died too soon or a cherished
colleague. Mortality checks to the left and to the right
of you, love dying in the frozen food aisle and
beginning at the checkout line. Hunger that begins
with a first cry, that remains with a full belly
and a ziploc full of crunchy goldfish ready at the bus
stop. Hunger for knowledge, for meaning to the
endlessness of tasks and parking spots and music
in the pouring rain and heartache. It can be almost
too much to bear, even the joy of it until our beloved
millennial lifts her head from her phone and says
she will be right with us and ends her endless game
of solitaire or wordle and with a toss of her hair
over her one eye showing she hands you an envelope
meant for another customer, 20 copies of shiny faces
of another, happier, well dressed family, faces
indecipherable from one another and yet somehow
even from your own.

Kelly J. Powell is a poet native to Long Island and a graduate of SUNY Binghamton's Creative Writing Program in 1988. She runs a reading series at bj spoke gallery in Huntington and has performed widely on Long Island and NYC. She also has a long standing commitment as a single mother to an amazing transgender college senior. She is at work now on a new book of poems called Posthumously Yours.

Pearl Ketover Prilik

Hunger

I'm hungry to cease
growling tiny bellies
to soothe aching stomachs
of mothers who go without
I'm hungry with a salivating
starve for the sanity of
salvation's sharing slipping
easily from those who have
any to those who have none

Dr. Pearl Ketover Prilik -poet/writer/psychoanalyst believes poetry captures life in a way that eludes linear language. PKP has been writing poetry since early childhood and is widely published. Living on the barrier island of south shore Long Island, NY, USA with DJ, her husband extraordinaire and Oliver, the humanoid cat, she continues to write because she simply has no other choice in the matter. More on PKP at "Imagine" http://drpkp.com

Patricia Rossi

The Gift

A single word

Without exception, it was always the same exact word

Spoken in a gentle whisper

Her response.... steadfast

My query..... annual

"What would you like for Christmas, Mom?"

The question posed, the answer given were metaphorically tucked in the eaves of our attic, packed in a corrugated box marked "Christmas Decorations"

As my Mother and I unwrapped and excavated fragile ornaments from crumpled newspaper, so too exhumed, our inevitable yuletide exchange

As the years tumbled into decades, I grew to truly understand my Mother's unwavering one word answer.

Now.............I too long for the very same gift

My Mother's annual monosyllabic reply...........PEACE.

Patricia Rossi is a publisher writer. Her narrative essays, poems and academic articles have been featured in newspapers, magazines, literary and scholarly journals nationally and internationally.

A. A. Rubin

Dealing With Rejection

I send my verses to the world,
And some of them find homes,
But what to do with all the rest,
Returned, rejected poems?

I send my stories swiftly out,
To journals far and wide—
But what to with ones against,
Which editors decide?

Mayhap collect them in a book;
Bind them in a tome,
And read them on some stormy night,
When I am all alone?

A. A, Rubin surfs the cosmos on winds of dark energy. His work has appeared recently in Love Letters to Poe, Ahoy! Comics, and Cowboy Jamboree. He can be reached on social media as @TheSurrealAri, or through his website, www.aarubin.com.

Robert Savino

Victory Garden

An old gardener, I clear a bed of earth
to scatter seeds and irrigate until dark.
Hope resonates with changing calendar pages
as moon shadows give way to sunlit days.

If only one flower breaks ground,
I am satisfied.

And when I open my lips to a new day
and only one person hears my joy,
I am satisfied.

But if the flowerbed opens in petals of plenty
around the outskirts of ready-to-pick vegetables,
it's like nothing I've felt before . . .

and I commit myself to feed multitudes.

Robert Savino, Suffolk County Poet Laureate 2015-2017, is a native Long Island poet, Board Member at the Walt Whitman Birthplace and Long Island Poetry & Literature Repository Center. He is the winner of the 2008 Oberon Poetry Prize. Robert is co-editor of two bilingual collections of Italian Americans Poets, *No Distance Between Us*. His books include *fireballs of an illuminated scarecrow, Inside a Turtle Shell* and *I'm Not the Only One Here.*

SCHEDAR

Amber Moon

Amber Moon, so full
please be still,
do not continue to rise
for the strength of your pull
will command the tears
to break free from the
lonely corners of my eye

Amber Moon,
stay where you are
don't let our distance
make me reach too far,
While getting sleepy
on the sand,
the eve lays you to rest
upon the palm of my hand

Amber Moon,
the sweet harvest
that feeds my soul
the mystery of
your orange glow
never grows old

Emily-Sue Sloane

High Fives

Yellow-eyed owl grounded,
caught in a net meant to
snag errant baseballs
in season at the high school.

One groundskeeper
strokes the raptor's brow,
repeating words of comfort
Good boy. You are beautiful, Bud.

His partner's gloved hands
work the netting away
from wing and talons curled
around tethering strands.

The men gently turn the owl over.
Go on, you're ok … They watch
as the daytime hunter
spreads its wings and disappears
without a backward glance.

Emily-Sue Sloane (emilysuesloane.com) is an award-winning Huntington Station, NY -based poet who writes to capture moments of wonder, worry and human connection. She is the author of a full-length poetry collection, *We Are Beach Glass* (2022), and her poems have been published in a variety of journals and anthologies.

Barbara Southard

Recipes In Time Of Famine
from several news articles 2008

If you take mud—mix well,
add butter, some salt, form into patties
then bake in the sun, you'd be surprised

how it calms down the stomach, takes
away pain. For variation—a bit of lemon,
something salvaged from the dump.

We think up new ways

like boiling water, telling our children that food
is almost ready
hope they'll fall asleep.

Then there's always skins and bones of dead animals

scattered about.

We gather them up, make a pot of soup.

Barbara Southard has served on the board of The Long Island Poetry Collective for many years. She's a short story writer, poet, & visual artist, and served as Suffolk County Poet Laureate from 2019-2021. She Lives in Miller Place, New York.

Allison Teicher-Fahrbach

Breathe

There is a better way
It is not just about survival anymore
It is a brand new day

Keep negativity at bay
Maybe it is time to adapt
There is a better way

Let the waves come as they may
You can only control your thoughts
It is a brand new day

This life is yours, so stay
And move out of the shadows
There is a better way

Do not walk away
It may be hard, though
It is a brand new day

Not all colors fade to gray
Look to the rising sun—
There is a better way
It is a brand new day

Allison Teicher-Fahrbach is an educational leader who is passionate about the fields of somatics and multilingualism. Her fifth book, *Darkness, to Light*, was published in 2023. She is working on a number of different education-related projects and plans to defend her doctoral dissertation about trauma-informed education in late 2023. More information about her work can be found at: www.solutionsforsouls.com.

Gayl Teller

Traveling in Arizona

Come along with me, meet Mary—
drive past the rattlesnake desert,
the jumping chollas that can surprise attack
and spring their spines deep under your too-close skin,
and even deeper when you try to resist,
like the Russian soldiers going deeper
and deeper into their neighboring Ukrainians,
head past the bleeding mass shootings,
the Covid virus going deeper and deeper into kin.

Come along with me, meet Mary,
a skinny, octogenarian lady, a free-hearted
smile on her wrinkly, leathery skin—
it will be worth the trip into merciless sun—
come down from the cooler Mount Lemon,
get past the mansions embedded in stone
of millionaire homes overlooking spectacular views,
come down to the foothills of the Catalina Mountains,
gaze across the fingering saguaro sands,
the orange-red Mexican birds of paradise— yes, I know,
so pretty!—and try to forego for now
the striking red cathedral rocks of Sedona.
Come on, keep up, come along with me
on these bumpy, tumbleweed tangled, sand strips,
where you hope your tires get a firm grip.

Come along with me, meet Mary,

as she lifts a rickety latch, lets you in
to the baked, bristly brown, harsh land
of the sanctuary, where makeshift wire mesh
and jury-rigged slats of wood, ropes
and carpet scraps shape ramshackle illusion,
for these pens she helped build are long-term homes,
where Mary has taken her patient, willing ascent
into giving. It's been 21 years now, 7 days a week
that Mary thinks of the life of a pig,
and here, there are 650 pigs she has helped rescue.

Come along with me, meet Mary,
as she takes off her long-sleeved overshirt,
soaks it in a rusty tub and puts it on,
dripping down her leathery brown legs,
bends herself in half to wrap Millie in a wet sheet,
points out beyond eyesight Babe's raised back hairs
are her hankering for a rubdown with Mary's touch
of gentleness, which Mary gives while whispering
softly into Babe's ear, Babe's name, again and again,
as you and I can begin again and again
to learn what it means to be fully, where
human renewal is found, here, here.

Come along with me, meet Mary,
as we walk and talk and she shares
their names, their beauty clear in her eyes,
as she relates their rescue stories,
like Blackie who lost his ear to a dog,
and Jo-Jo who lost her eye to a viral bug,
and Sylvester who lost his cuteness to a pet owner.

Come along with me, meet Mary,

who pulls the rug out from under pig myths,
so "eating like a pig," in truth, she laughs,
means "they eat only a cupful, no more,"
who spends her all with love and enthusiasm,
one of a kind, meet Mary, who helps us
see unlearning is the road to learning,
and look for Mary wherever you travel.

Gayl Teller, former Nassau County Poet Laureate and 2016 Walt Whitman Birthplace Poet of the Year, is author of 7 poetry collections, most recently, *Flashlight: New and Selected Poems* (Cherry Grove/ Word Tech, 2019), and editor of two poetry anthologies, *Toward Forgiveness* (Writers Ink)--awarded a NY State Decentralization Grant for the Arts, and *Corona* (Walt Whitman Birthplace Assn.). Nationally and internationally acclaimed, she directs the Mid-Island Y Poetry Series and teaches at Hofstra University.

Tracy L. Thompson

Semi-Sweet Morsel

Her love is flawless
and I am worthy of it without cause.
She holds no grudge, even when I say no.
I'm sure I've said no.
Like me, she is easily distracted
by the promise of something more interesting.
She indulges our endless requests to perform
her most-recently-acquired amazing talent.
We marvel at her goings out and her comings in.
We cannot believe our great good fortune.
And sometimes, she bites.

Tracy L. Thompson is a poet and writer currently working from Schenectady, NY. She is grateful to have never known hunger, and grief-stricken over a world where children go to bed hungry while billionaires fly rocketships to Mars. She loves her family and her dogs above all things. She is working on her first novel, "Out Like a Lion."

John Jay Tucker

Boomer

Funny

By the time
We turn sixty

All we really have
Is time for friendship

But some are
Still to busy for naps

Maybe by sixty-five
We'll catch up

And have conversations
About simple situations

Pressed with I don't knows
Stuck on these or that's

Heads still filled
With tons of crap

By seventy
We'll hold our breath

And realize its

A decade since we've
Been quite harmless

Seventy-five is the big surprise
Which truly settles spirit

The next years could
Be cold and lonesome

Eighty is a strong year for
Remembering everything

Eighty-five
Is all about the weather

Steady wind and rains
Our very best of friends

While ninety
Is a wish list country

Hopeful we'll all get to visit

A husband, father and grandfather while in retirement enjoys substitute teaching at Lawrence Woodmere Academy, yoga, hiking and attending poetry events. Published in PPA Literary Reviews 20-25, Bards Annual 2020-21, Nassau County Voices In Verse 2022

J R Turek

Random Acts
for Chip

No fanfare, no headlines
or breaking news alert, just a heart
reaching out in support, in encouragement,
silent as quarters dropped in an expired meter
for a stranger, paying for the family of five
standing behind you on line at Arby's
calculating what they could and couldn't
afford to eat, holding back horn honking traffic
for a runaway dog/cat/squirrel/duck
to safely cross the roadway.

No reason to trumpet these actions,
these random acts of kindness flow
through with little time spent
rationalizing good deeds, a natural
part of someone whose joy is abundant.
I love hearing and reading about these gifts,
recipients bubbly with amazement
that these people do their thing. I wish,
oh how I wish, there were more givers
for more receivers to praise.

And then I met you.
No heavenly choir sang out your name,
no red carpet or paparazzi parade when
we met, no reason to think you were shielding

your angelic wings behind you. I didn't wear
a sign that said I need help, didn't take out
an ad that I was in over my head, couldn't find
answers to my questions on red alert deadline.

There you were, offering not a handout
not a pity party guilt-trip do-a-good-deed
today because someone might be watching,
no thought to time or inconvenience or degree
of difficulty involved to assist me.
You. Just. Did. And now I know that it's
what you do, how your soul reaches across
despair to bring a smile and relief. My gratitude
is sunbursts of gladness.

Maybe it's no big deal to you but for me,
it's mountains more than that. No, not random
that you were there to take on my problem
as your own, tenacious to keep at it when I
had given up for the thousandth time, no,
nothing random. I saw the fingers of your soul
reach out, felt them touch my cheek, invited them
to rest a while in my heart where I can reach in
and reach out to someone in need, following
your lead... no no no, nothing random about it.

J R (Judy) Turek, Superintendent of Poetry for the LI Fair, 2020 Hometown Hero, 2019 LI Poet of the Year, Bards Laureate 2013-2015, editor, mentor, workshop leader, and author of seven poetry books, the most recent *Dog-Speak* is supporting North Shore Animal League, the *world's* largest no-kill shelter. 'The Purple Poet' has written a poem a day for 19 years; she lives on Long Island with her soul-mate husband, Paul, her dogs, and her extraordinarily extensive shoe collection. msjevus@optonline.net

James P. Wagner (Ishwa)

Hashbrown Mathematics

During some semesters of my college years,
I spent my mornings working a shift,
At a drive-thru convenience store,
To make a few extra bucks.
No mathematical way to "pay my way,"
Through college…
But maybe enough afford an odd textbook or two.
Part of my unofficial duties on the morning shift,
Was to go to the deli across the street,
And pick up breakfast orders for me and my co-worker.
It was a good deli, with good food,
And mostly good workers…
Mostly…

One unsuspecting morning, I get on line
And a rather husky, somewhat overweight gruff guy,
Is ready to take my order…
"Hey can I help you?" He asks.
"Yeah, I'll take two BEC sandwiches, salt, pepper, ketchup,
and two sides of hashbrowns…"
"So, four hashbrowns?"
I look confused. "Two SIDEs of hashbrowns."
"So, that's four hashbrowns, right?"
"How many come in a side of hashbrowns?"
"Two!"
"So yeah, two of those…"
"So that would be four hashbrowns total?"

"Do we order them individually?"

"No."

"Ok then…so yes, I guess it would be four total hashbrowns, but two sides, one for me, and one for someone else…"

"So that's two sides, of four hashbrowns?"

Almost ready to pull a looney toons and have my eyes pop out of their sockets, I do everything I can to hold back a scream.

"Whatever comes in a side of hashbrowns, whether its 1, 2, 3, or 4 hashbrowns, give me TWO of those, two sides of hashbrowns, if its 2 hashbrowns, in each side, then yes, make 4 total, for TWO sides!"

"Ok…" he says and saunters off to the back.

I noticed a patron waiting on line next to me had overheard
And was laughing at my predicament.

"Is what I asked really that complicated?" I asked him.

He smiled and shook his head "No…no it wasn't."

"Thank you…Id like to do the math on how this guy got this job…"

Another patron chimed in:

"He's the owner's brother…"

"Ah," I said. "Well, that adds up."

Margarette Wahl

Losing and Receiving

Once green will be brown
then dead to the ground.
A leaf will not fall vibrant shades of yellow this Autumn.
A drought has sucked it's moisture and life out like my tears I have shed for
you.

Some days everything's dead and gone.

Through all this sadness
trenches of crunching madness
a moment to be grateful for,
to have known you.

Sometimes the people we love become our most precious treasures.

In a time to give
an imperishable item
a piece of clothing
a crumpled dollar bill
a thought
a prayer
a phone call
to donate in your memory.

Today I gave blood.

Margarette Wahl is a Special Ed Teacher Aide for twenty-one years and a member of Bards, PPA, and an advisor on the NCPLS. Her poetry muses are her crushes, cats, friends, & people she associates with.

Herb Wahlsteen

Lose All the Blues

Mama keeps on crying,
buying the kids new shoes.
Papa keeps on sighing,
dying from evening news:

with so much madness,
hey, what a bad mess,
say, what plan can
lose all the blues.

Me, I'm here copin',
hopin' I will survive.
My hands are open,
gropin' to stay alive.

Yesterday's a mem'ry,
tomorrow's just a dream,
and today's a bent tree
sorrowin' in a stream.

Singers go on singing,
bringing a brief relief.
Music keeps on ringing,
lingering through our grief:

with so much madness,
hey, what a bad mess,

say, what plan can
lose all the blues.

Me, I'm here copin',
hopin' I will survive.
My hands are open,
gropin' to stay alive.

Yesterday's a mem'ry,
tomorrow's just a dream,
and today's a bent tree
sorrowin' in a stream.

Herb Wahlsteen earned a B.A. in English from CA. St. U., Fullerton, and an M. A. in English from Columbia U. He then worked many years as a high school teacher in New York City Public Schools. He was a finalist in the Yale Series of Younger Poets contest (1989, Adam and Eve in the 20th Century, James Merrill, judge), placed 3rd in the Writer's Digest 77th Annual Writing Competition: Rhyming Category, and has had poems published in: *Long Island Quarterly, the Great South Bay Magazine, The Long Islander, The Lyric* magazine, *Paumanok Interwoven, Paumanok Transition, Suffolk County Poetry Review, Bards Annual, Form Quarterly, Bards Against Hunger, 13 Days of Halloween, Poets to Come, The Hands We Hold, A Tree in a Garden of Ashes, Beat Poets Anthology, String Poet* (2 poems translated from the French, 2 poems translated from the Spanish), *Pratik; A Magazine of Contemporary Writing*, and *Measure* magazine.

Mary Winters

conklin barn

 tonight I sit in conklin barn, listen
while poets sing pieces for peace
and try to change the world

surrounded by wires, amps
and microphones
long-haired musicians strum
acoustic guitars, sing
ambiguous lyrics

now and then I catch
a distinctive metaphor
bounce off a rough wooden wall

amidst these youngsters
who mimic our ways, our days
and think they discovered them
I feel old
old as this barn
standing strong with a history

ancient rafters look down on
peace-sign pamphlets
a musician sits on a wooden cube
bangs a beat while a cellist plays

I watch music and poetry hold hands

and think about my generation
with its music, ideas, and protests
we were tough in our fight for peace

now, like the old barn I look upon
these young idealists
see them fight for their future
their children's future
as we fought for ours
I'm proud of the path we've paved

above the blaring music
in them I hear the sound
of generations past

Mary Winters is a Long Island, New York poet who has been writing poetry since 2004. Mary is a member of the Farmingdale Poetry Group, the Farmingdale Creative Writing Group, and the Long Island Writer's Guild. In 2005, she won Honorable mention for her poem "Elegy of a Slave Girl" in the Lake Ronkonkoma Historical Society poetry contest.

Thomas Zampino

All These Things Are Broken

all these things are broken
and I was once the man to fix them
but I'm older now, and tired too
and there will always be more
to fix, so I'll let them be, just like
me (broken has its place)

Thomas Zampino, a Manhattan attorney for over 35 years, started writing poetry only recently (https://gracepending.wordpress.com/). Some of his works have appeared in The University of Chicago's *Memoryhouse Magazine*, *Silver Birch Press* (twice), *Bard's Annual 2019, 2020, and 2021*, *Trees in a Garden of Ashes*, *Otherwise Engaged*, *Chaos, A Poetry Vortex*, *Nassau County Voices in Verse*, and *No Distance Between Us*. A video enactment of his poem *Precise Moment* was produced by Brazilian director and actor Gui Agustini. His first book of poetry, *Precise Moment*, was published in 2021. His second book, synchronicity, was published in 2023 by Southern Arizona Press. He is from New York.

VIRGINIA

Dennis Barnes

Solitary Confinement

Dad's favorite chair
is tucked in a corner,
where he wastes away
like a prisoner
confined to a cell
with no bars
serving out his sentence
swallowing pills,
watching television,
stumbling to the bathroom.

We appeal his sentence,
this life in this cushy prison,
to a series of doctors
who shake their heads
much like Dad now does
when we ask how can we help.
Out of nowhere Dad requests
a fishing rod, yet when
placed in his hand,
there is no recognition.

The blue chair confines
Dad as he rages
against boredom
sitting there in between
so much time before

and so much time after,
knowing that he
and the chair will soon
dissolve into dust
and be freed.

Dennis Barnes lives in Northern Virginia where he leads a not-so-quiet poetic life. He was the 2005 recipient of the Baltimore People's Poetry *Done the Most to Advance Poetry* award. Mr. Barnes has had poems published in over forty magazines and anthologies. *Shades of Light*, his first book of poetry, was published in 2007.

Mike Croghan

Wayfinding

The middle territory between
Stuck and
                        Lost
is so very vast
and wise
and free.
And yet...

The wicked gravity
of those twin poles -
those deep and greedy
wells of seduction -
(those two edges
of the same perilous
sword)
is almost
irresistible.

We've killed plenty of time,
you and I,
stuck in Stuck or
                lost in Lost,
going nowhere.
But perhaps
that was always
part
of the path.

Mike Croghan works with code by day, which has more in common with poetry than you might think. Mike's first poetry chapbook, *Body and Soul*, was published by Local Gems Press in 2018. You can read more of his work at freesourfruit.com.

Ladi Di

Broke Not Broken

No where to lay
No where to rest
No where to lay her head
No bed to sleep
Standing on meridian...
 Fear deep
A few inches from busy street
A mighty mighty long time
 Since she had any food to eat
Appreciating opened bottle of
 Water...helping to combat her
 Serious thirst and intense heat.
An act of kindness
An act of Love
A show of care...her sunken eyes
 Reveal eminent look of despair
But for Grace of God, I go there.
She turned completely...quickly
 Walked away
Turned back around...
Looked deeply into my eyes
 To say God bless you
You are only person who gave me
 Something today!
Sign she carried read
 "Broke Not Broken".

Sylvia Dianne Beverly is an Internationally acclaimed poet, presenting poetry in London, England, at the Lewisham Theater. A collection of her work is housed at George Washington University's Gelman Library. Ladi Di, as she is affectionately called is a proud member of Poets on the Green Line, Poetry X Hunger, Poetry Poster Project and Voices of Woodlawn. She celebrated the 40th Anniversary of Host Grace Cavalieri, reading on her show "The Poet and the Poem" at the Library of Congress Experience. She is a founding member of the Anointed PENS (Poets Empowered to Nurture Souls) Poetry Ministry, out of Ebenezer AME Church, an alum of Poets in Progress with Poet Laureate of District of Columbia, the late Dolores Kendrick.

Anne Emerson

Leaving the Land

Why do people move
to some cities?
Dazzling lights; derided farms?
Glamor, grit, or glory?

Buses – threading throngs
walking on the tarmac –
carry riders on roofs,
or hanging from windows;
filling rear platforms – feet within,
torsos swaying outward,
single hands holding on.

On the sidewalk, a woman lying –
eyes crusted white;
black rags hanging loose
around skin that barely covers bones;
two small coins in a cup beside her;
passers-by stepping
over and around her.

Amid dry and dusty desert dunes,
a taxi slows, arriving at the pyramids.
Many hands slap and stick onto its windows –
hands of pre-teen boys
who crowd and breathe on tourists
exiting the taxi: "Buy mine! Buy mine!"

Why?
People pour into cities from cities
as much as from farms;
many movers choose city or oil field
over farm or nomads' desert.

Does land lack a living?
Why do cities grow and give homes,
but land does not?

Anne Emerson was born in England and travelled to North Africa many years ago. She has never forgotten her observations there. She lives in Virginia with her husband of 45 years; her poems have been published in NoVA Bards, and The Poets' Domain.

Cathy Hailey

Vantage Point

Each summer as July approached, we were drawn to the city:
as a child, with parents and younger brother—energized by the crowds,
as a teen, with friends, boyfriends—celebrating our independence,
as parents, introducing our new family to the haunts of our pasts.

The heat of July, the hub of DC, picnicking in red, white and blue,
soaking in the sun, dodging the red of burn, dancing to popular tunes
as we awaited nightfall and the kaleidoscope of colors blasting the sky
as fireworks boomed and the nation united in collective celebration.

The vantage point didn't matter—
a picnic blanket directly under the Washington Monument, circled by flags,
on the Lincoln Memorial stairs, under the gaze of a seated President,
at the carousel of circling horses beside the Hirshhorn's sculpture garden,

the roof of Casa Maria Restaurant nestled in the waterfront fish market,
Lady Bird Johnson Park across the Potomac, short walk from the Pentagon,
Gravelly Point Park under descending planes headed to National,
atop the hill on Arlington Ridge Road overlooking Pentagon City—

What will these views bring post COVID 19? Post January 6th Insurrection?
Post Fascist and authoritarian leanings? Post increased White Supremacy?
Uprisings of Anti-Black, Latinx, Asian, Jew, Muslem, Woman, LGBTQ+,
Anti-humanity, intellectualism, literature, education? Post Hate for the sake
of Hate?

Cathy Hailey teaches in Johns Hopkins University's MA in Teaching Writing program and previously taught high school English and Creative Writing. She is Northern Region Vice President of The Poetry Society of Virginia and organizes In the Company of Laureates. Her chapbook, I'd Rather Be a Hyacinth, was published by Finishing Line Press.

Nick Hale

Maria

They gave you a rosary
when you became a woman:
a life raft in a sea of sin.
Sterling and stone -your stone-
engraved "salve Maria."

Your fine riches,
with these,
how will I made it
into heaven?
made them laugh.

You'd clutch tight
each night
search for forgiveness,
to understand each contour
falling asleep on it,
leaving little bead marks
on your breast, or cheek, or shoulder.

Somewhere in the years,
the raft became an anchor
tethered to routine.
Before it drowned you, you cast
it to me; a life raft in this sea of sin
to keep me afloat long enough to join you.

Nick Hale is the founder and leader of NoVA Bards and the Northern Virginia Poetry Group. He is a co-founder and the current vice president of the Bards Initiative, a Long Island based poetry nonprofit. Formerly both a literal and metaphorical hat collector, these days, Nick only collects metaphorical hats. He is a partner, publisher, editor, and author with Local Gems Press and has worked on several anthologies including the best-selling *Sound of Solace*. In addition to writing, editing, and performing poetry, Nick enjoys teaching poetry and has given several seminars, panels, and workshops on various poetic topics. In his own poetry, he often enjoys humor and experimenting with different styles, which may make him seem, at times, like he has yet to find his voice. A former almost-teacher, Nick earned a BA in English and an M.Ed in Secondary Education before deciding he didn't want to teach, teaching himself the basics of IT and web design, and then doing neither of those things. Along with James P. Wagner, Nick co-authored *Japanese Poetry Forms: A Poet's Guide*. He is the author of *Broken Reflections* and three upcoming chapbooks which, he claims haven't been published yet only because he's too busy working on books that are not his.

K. A. Lewis

Tree Anemone

Airy anemone
I see by touch
breeze trembling across
a thousand origami
leaves at once

Birds flutter cling
flocking in my hair chirp
peep cheep hop hopping
tiny claws on skin bark
scritch prickle sing

Eat light follow
sun exhale oxygen
ask rain to fall flip
leaves upside down
pale beseeching palms

I scrub heaven
bow toss and comb gales
thousand fingered hands flirt
lightening charged atoms
tickle my bones

Drink deep wet earth
guzzle seeking roots
sap a river rising

wind roaring
I sieve life

K. A. Lewis graduated from the Corcoran School of Art in 1986 with little idea of how to make a living. Her work experience includes cake decoration, jewelry sales, hypnosis certification, being robbed at gunpoint, and 32 years as a custom picture framer. Since 2014, her poetry and genre fiction have been published in several anthologies. Katy and her husband live with four demanding cats in a small book-stuffed house in Falls Church, VA.

Megan McDonald

Reading poetry prompts without glasses

Reading poetry prompts without glasses
causes problems as I was wanting to cook
a typical weekend meal
with whipped mashed potatoes
oh God I realized
that I was riding on a wrong word
that it was crooked not cooking or cooked
I was deeply disappointed
that the poem has to askew
from where I was going
with ripe tomatoes
dizzying good asparagus
aromatic herbs to be planted
if I'm wise I will stick with
red tomatoes to be simmered
long and slow and not punish
myself with trying to write
a crooked poem aaaaaa
I give in to the farmers market
to delight in the abundance
and decide to go with cooking
crooked can wait for another day
besides there is a request
for beer braised bratwurst
with cucumber tomato salad

there is no need to do
a pre-ordered Escher style poem
this week so I'll stick with
ripe words waiting to be harvested

Betty Jo Middleton

Blessings on the Hungry

Blessings on the hungry:
the children who whimper
and cry in the night,
the mothers who never
have quite enough to eat,
the fathers who will do
almost anything
to feed their hungry family,
the young adult
without enough money
to go to the grocery store and
with too much pride
to go to the food bank.

Betty Jo Middleton is the author of Senior Moments: Poems. "On a Bright Sunday Morning" about John Lewis was in a virtual visual exhibit "Speak Your Truth/Black Lives Matter." She lives in Alexandria, Virginia, where her poems have appeared on DASH busses. "The Goose That Laid the Tarnished Egg" won first place in Poets Roundtable of Arkansas August 2022 contest.

Susan Notar

Ode to a Grapefruit

I gently wash the rosy-colored skin, slice
it in two circular sections: pink pulpy fruit.
I place it gently in my favorite French bowl
and delight in the agility of spoon
scooping flesh my tongue tasting tangy juices.
Such deceptively simple pleasures we share.
Next to me another's coffee cup awaits
the morning paper crisp the front page full of drear.
I turn to the horoscope and Travel instead.
Mexican ruins? The Côte d'Azur? Venice?
For now, perhaps more grapefruit, coffee, *sugar.*

Susan Notar has flown over Iraq in helicopters wearing body armor and makes a mean beurre blanc sauce. She is a Pushcart-prize nominated poet whose work has appeared in a number of publications including *Gyroscope*, *Burningword*, *Artemis*, *Written in Arlington*, T*he Bridgewater Review*, *Penumbra*, *The Poet: Stand with Ukraine*, *Joys of the Table: An Anthology of Culinary Verse*, *Penumbra*, and *NoVA Bards*. She works for the U.S. State Department helping vulnerable communities in the Middle East.

Phyllis Price

A Capella
after Gethsemane

I browse through heady volumes
in the bookshop, read a line or two
from a book on the desert fathers,
consider arid solitude,
how drought could calm
unquiet currents in me.

Morse code from a friar's cane
pelts uneven cobblestones,
robe uplifted by an errant breeze,
brogans run down at the heels,
his pace propelled by habit,
constancy of vows.

The chapel sends a chill,
sterility of stone and wood
to quell desire of more than
ora et labora. At 12 the chants begin.
My sternum hums--no longer bone--
the composition, foreign yet familiar.

Phyllis Price's work appears in the chapbook **Quarry Song** and journals *Appalachian Heritage, Pine Mountain Sand and Gravel, Poem, Connecticut River Review, Anthology of Appalachian Writers*, and others. Her focus is the natural world and man's relationship to it. Price resides on a small farm in Southwest Virginia.

Tamara Priestley

To Teach

To teach is not to preach.
The professor and the pupil, each
Must discover daily lessons, given
For absolute knowledge, hidden.

The professor and the pupil, each
Imparting puzzle pieces, reach
For absolute knowledge, hidden.
Guided by the other, trust

Imparting puzzle pieces, reach
For true enlightenment, being
Guided by the other; trust:
To teach is not to preach.

Tamara Priestley is a teacher of English learners at Jamestown High School in Williamsbur.

K.S. Taylor-Barnes

Obscurity

Looking through glass
that magnifies the living,
he watches others fill their days
with laughter and memories,
while he sits alone,
a quiet aching in his soul
to be part of
all he sees
knowing that,
for him,
this time has passed.
So, he sits…
Waiting for the day to end.
Watching his family.
Longing to be awakened
from this world of obscurity
and reconnected
with those who revere him
as a giant among men
while he fights to remain
part of the living.
Happy to sit.
Content to watch
through his tethered lenses
life as it was
and will never be again.

K.S. Taylor-Barnes (Kathy) is a native Virginian, retired Fairfax County high school English teacher, mother of five, and grandmother of nine. She is a member of NoVA Bards and the Poetry Society of Virginia. Kathy was previously published in the 2021, 2022 and 2023 NoVa Bards anthologies as well as Poets Anonymous *Gathering* and will soon be published in the *Loch Raven Review.* Kathy's first chapbook, *From Light into Darkness,* poems that chronicle the brief life of her daughter, was recently printed by Local Gems Press.

Lesley Tyson

skipping lunch

i hadn't planned to skip lunch
but today accelerated too quickly
i grabbed the mail-club gourmet chocolate bar
delivered in Monday's rain
only to realize the summer occurred
over the weekend somewhere
between Brooklyn and Virginia

the melted resolidified dark chocolate
feels as chalky as it tastes
the pink ocean salt washed out to sea
in the overflow of a scalding thunderstorm

From Reston, Virginia, has had work in issues of several Virginia anthologies. Lesley is also co-editor of several other anthologies. Lesley's first book of poetry: *journey through red heaven* was released in 2019. She also has two mini-chapbooks: *what never changes* and *a stone in the rain-49 haiku*. Lesley is a regular contributor to several local Northern Virginia poetry groups and co-leads Poets Anonymous ©, Northern Virginia's longest running open reading.

CONNECTICUT

Adele Evershed

Goingness

I'll be gone in the night
Or into the habit forming silence
With a flooded flourish
Every real human element behind me
You think you can move me to
Another time zone
But the stars are always wasted
And the Instagram gargoyles dying

The children live on
Though they were declared dead on arrival
Yet you have painted over
Slaughtered babies in the snow before
Substituting dogs or other animals
And you choose to see little of the fall
Leaving carcasses on the beach
As you go to lunch

Disbelief expressed through a single word
Repeats like your heart beat
Pumping blood and holding up your body
You depend on quick pick me ups
Coffee in Styrofoam
Your storms in a D-cup
Turmoil in limited characters
And your only protest printed on a T-shirt

Maybe the gentle voice will survive
Pointing out where the breaks will be
More likely the poet will write about goingness
And be called fake news
Her body of work trashed
Even though she admitted at the outset
Nothing she said would hold back the change
For even a single second

Adele Evershed was born in Wales and now lives in Wilton, Connecticut. Her prose and poetry have been published in over a hundred online journals and print anthologies. Adele has been nominated for the Pushcart Prize and Best of the Net for poetry, and her first poetry chapbook, Turbulence in Small Spaces was published this year by Finishing Line Press.

Gloria Jainchill

Hunger

Years ago as I watched TV
Saw hungry children of the 3rd world
I stopped, thankful and prayed
They would have food another day.

Got a job, earned my own money
Gave some to the Feed The Children charities
Ate every morsel on my plate
There were starving children in the world.

Married divorced with children of my own
I needed to feed them good food.
Housing costs clothes school supplies
And times not enough money for food, I cried.

Learned the pain hunger could bring
But not the sting and numbness of continual hunger
Remembered times parents had no money for food
Children hungry but Society of Vincent De Paul came through.

Learned the number of U. S. children
Who go to bed hungry each night
Food deprivation too close to home for me
Began giving food to local food pantries.

As a senior citizen
We have a great senior center in town

Eyes opened wider seeing more senior hunger
I give proteins and other essentials, to local food pantry.

For $3.00 seniors can get a full noontime meal
Monday through Friday at our senior center.
We are thankful for these healthy meals
That helps us make ends meet at the end of the month.

I think about how lucky I am
To live in this beautiful Glastonbury town
Our senior center was an uphill battle
But now a life saver for us seniors in town.

Medical bills broken cars and plumbing leaks
Ate up my social security check and savings.
Playing cards, Wii bowling and $3.00 lunches
Is how I make ends meet.

September is senior month and Fight Against Hunger Poetry Anthology.
Many thoughts swirl about my head and roar
I lift prayers for us all, the fight against hunger,
Homeland and world peace, to end violence and killing of each other.

Gloria began writing poetry at age 7 while playing school with her younger brother who was recovering from Polio. Thus began a lifelong love for poetry. Gloria has self-published several poetry books, *Love Shines In Darkness, My Glastonbury Poetry, and Poetry Is Fun,* a book she co-authored with her granddaughter to help her process her grief when her elementary school closed in 2018.

Patti Barker Kierys

Listen To Your Heart

The messages of your heart
stop, listen, hear and receive
what they offer to help you be
living a joyous and exciting life

Go beyond your safe space

do not let fear stop you
you will receive and let go to live
whatever you wish and dream
Say no to your inner critic

it does not serve you in any way
your heart knows what you need
listen to its whispering messages
Heart messages will guide you

enjoy the ride, be with it
surprises need not be fearful
let them be joyful and hopeful

Your heart holds great wisdom
share it with those who care
they are waiting to know you
special people are here to stay

Your heart's joy lets you know
you are and never were alone
listen for spirit always remains
there is still much to say and do

Patti Barker Kierys is a woman of many interests. She is an award wining artist, Reiki Master Teacher, author, poet and photographer. Her creative passion and spiritual inspiration can be seen in her poems, paintings, collage, photography and inspirational messages. She has been practicing Reiki for over twenty years. She writes articles for the international organization Reiki Rays. Upon retiring after 50 years in law, a surprising passion arose. She began writing poetry and continues to enjoy it to this day. Several of her poems have been published. She can be reached at pmkierys@att.com and on Facebook - Patti Barker Kierys

Tom Lagasse

Our Daily Bread

I
Give us this day
merely enough to witness
the last kiss
of autumnal sunlight
on the steeple.

Give us this day
childlike splendor to play
as leaves rain down
on us, and we wear
like crowns.

II
Our daily bread
and perhaps a glass of wine
or a cup of tea warmed
on the hearth. The crust
softens as it sops the dregs
from the soup bowl.

Our daily bread
will be enough to be
satiated; yet the hunger
to be transformed by being
light enough to take
flight as though we

were born with wings.

III
And forgive us our trespasses
as we indulge in
these final days before
the winter when our bones
will be laid bare
of our transgressions
overflowing with gluttony
and hope.

And forgive us our trespasses
when our neighbors
needed to be seen
and who had faith
they would be fed
like those who sat
hungry on the mountain
when a few fishes and loaves
fed them all.
Our sin is believing
this was a different time.

IV
As we forgive those
who trespass against
us. Those who believe
life is Monopoly
and money tallies the score-
board, the difference
between winners and losers,
and the ego believes

the crowd will remember
how they played this game
like it was the 1954 World
Series which can only
be seen in black and white
and romanticized.

As we forgive those
who trespass against
us and to be freed
of the burden that is
the inherited bondage
that small thread
of DNA that separates
humans from the other
mammals.

V

And lead us not into
temptation where a world
of our own making blinds
the eye to greater powers
like gravity and the human
capacity to love.

And lead us not into
temptation where belief
and hope suffice. When
the world calls us to love
and asks more than light
romance but the deep act
of sacrificing one's life for
the other.

VI
But deliver us from evil
found in the dark hard-
hearted places: the politics
of power and the cynical act
of allowing corrosion
to transform into corruption's
rotting rust.

But deliver us from evil
with bravery to withstand
the attacks to see the tree
needs fungi and the fungi
rain and the rain sun
to cycle water like
a waterwheel.
Deliver us from evil.
Amen.

Tom's poetry has appeared in numerous anthologies and publications. By
day, he writes and gardens. By night, he works bringing spice to grocery
stores nationwide. He lives in Bristol, CT.

Patricia Martin

The Walk

First touch before first kiss
good little parochial school girl
new to menstruating
let alone wise to the ways of boys
instructed by my Irish Catholic mother
to walk the two miles to church
by myself
for Friday afternoon Lenten service

Perfect day for a walk
the sights so familiar
the curving road
pretty suburban houses
the smell of earth waking up
crocus and daffodils stretching up
the breeze fresh

No one was around
occasionally a car would pass by
or my Mary Janes would crunch a pebble
otherwise all was quiet
and solitary
I was feeling independent
enjoying the reverie
of my own little girl thoughts

One sloping hill away from town
and the sanctuary of St. John's
a boy walked toward me
I did not know him
He was cute
I was shy
and did not look at him

He drew closer
and on approach
suddenly veered to my side of the walkway
reached out
cradled my crotch in his hands
murmured something I could not quite hear
and kept going
As if
As if
As if
nothing was out of line
nothing was unusual
nothing was wrong

I kept going
not sure what had happened
not sure why my cheeks felt so hot
not sure why I felt ashamed
What had he said?
What was I to do?

I did not know
so I kept walking
my feet did not stop
I did not look back
and never told a single soul

Patricia Martin is an author, poet, performer/actor, and freelance writer/communications professional who has been featured at numerous venues, festivals, on radio and television, and published in various periodicals and anthologies. A member of the Author's Guild, The Nonfiction Author's Association, and The Connecticut Poetry Society, Martin is the author of six nonfiction books and a poetry collection, and collaborated on a CD with composer/producer/musician Gus Mancini. www.patriciamartin.com.

Nancy Noell

Who Cares?

We watch the News.
We are warned,
"These images may be disturbing:"
Covered bodies lying on the ground,
Children with no chance of full life,
A fallen bike—the biker's legs still
Wrapped around the seat and center bar—
Struck down in mid-stride;
A railroad station littered with suitcases, baby strollers,
Scattered clothing--detritus of the dead.
I look away but tell myself I must see.
The world must see!
A pregnant woman carried on a stretcher,
Holding her swollen belly.
Later news lets us know she gave birth
But lost her own life.
Who will care for her child?
Who cares for the injured?
The raped?
The dead?
The refugees escaped from the horror?
Who cries for the tragedies of war?
Who cares?

Nancy writes poetry, mainly focusing on nature and her surroundings. Her poetry has been published in Connecticut Barbs in 2019 and 2020. She is a retired teacher, now an avid gardener and lives with her husband in Gales Ferry, Connecticut.

Laura Saraniero

Petals

Wrested Carelessly diffused on the floor
 Sweet, soft, supple, healthy
Beautiful
Alone
Detached,
To g th er
Alone
You should be sad but, really
The flowers suffering their absences won't outlast them
At least not by much longer
Petals as fragrant and unmarred
At least not in the way you think
Standing in the absence of nothing
I breath deep
Regardless of my often chocked sinuses
Lower myself to the silken whispers tickling my face
Whispering tickles of my tips
Sliding up my hip
Secrets you need not know
Made no less by their sacred silence
To you
Your thoughts not mine
You don't need to see my brilliance
To qualify how bright I shine

Originally from Long Island, Laura Saraniero is now living in Ct, USA. She's been previously published in the Southwest Connecticut Bards Anthology from Local Gems and is continuously looking for homes for her work as well as local and virtual open mics to hook into.

Virginia Shreve

My Mother Wore Squash Blossoms in her Hair

Hit me over the head with a shovel
my mother told my brother
if I get too old and my mind elopes with the moon
and howls
and howls
and
howls.

If I am stuck in stutter-step-stutter
my mind stubbed in just stutter
Hit me over the head with a shovel
and tuck me snug among the zucchini.

No one will look for me there.

In August, neighbors cower
behind their doors fearful
of the vegetable albatross
left in bursting sacks on porches
afraid they will have to learn
how to make bread or birdhouses

Hit me over the head with a shovel
my mother told my brother
and leave me snug among the zucchini
You'll make a clean getaway

and so

will

I

Virginia Shreve, , the Town of Canton Poet Laureate and the Connecticut Beat Poet Laureate for 2020-2022, resides in a small river town in CT with husband and dogs, none well-trained, but all good-natured. For years she wrote and edited numerous regional newsletters, much dog humor, and her poems have appeared in print and online in The Southern Poetry Review, Naugatuck River Review, Slippery Elm, Phantom Drift, Your Daily Poem, and others, including various anthologies. Her poem "Tintype" was nominated for a Pushcart Prize.

PENNSYLVANIA

Mary Anne Abdo

Generational Poverty In Three Voices

Grandmother
Always the rebel hippie, playing the cool girl smoking a jay with the boys.
Finding myself pregnant after a night's fling.
Old-fashioned parents non-too pleased.
Kicking me out to sleep on that "friend's "couch.
Crying baby with diapers and no money.
Making myself comfortable in the welfare line.
Not knowing if we could survive.

        Daughter
        I am the product of a one night's stand.
        Angry with this situation.
        No mother was every at home.
        Never to guide me from this wretched world.
        Vodka being my choice of escaping.
        Hungry and alone…
        Bullied at school
        Because of no family for me at home.
        Hiding amongst the vale of shame.
        A sometimes visit from my grandparents.
        Social workers and street friends I guess are family.
        Sitting in a hospital bed just gave birth to a daughter.
        Waiting on a call from the county assistance office.
        And now where to go.

Granddaughter
I was born shaking from alcohol withdrawal.
Mom runs away from time to time.

Needing to escape from her pain.
Making sure I am never truly alone.
Grandma is more involved, she is ten years sober.
Taking me to school, soccer and ballet.
Mom just sits by and watches in a trance.
Angry and sad…
Probably wishing she had more of grandma than I have.
At least we eat dinner together.
I think life is getting slightly better.

Together
Sometimes we are dealt cards not of our own choosing.
Seeking emotional support and finding none.
Seeking food and shelter in a never-ending line of disgust.
Wondering when it will be our time.
Wondering why we did this or that.
Hoping though each generation life will be different

Mary Anne Abdo is an author, poet and photographer. With a background in freelance journalism; she uses her poetry as a source of creative expression, which reflects on many facets of what it means to be a human being living in these modern times. Her debut poetry book, "Fractured Lollipop Poems of Brokenness Healing and Hope is now on Amazon Follow Mary Anne on WordPress:
https://bluestainedglass.wordpress.com

Pamela Blanding-Godbolt

TODAY ~ The Blank Page

We are BLESSED DAILY with
The Blank Page
Not Often Recognized as Such
Familiar to us all as a Day . . .Today
The Journey, our Individual Paths
Often Clogged by Twist and Turns
Days with Moments of Stagnation
Our Next Moves Under Contemplation
Days Lived at a Snail's Pace
Oblivious to the Reality of Life as a Race
A Race in Time
As our Days' Are Numbered
Known only to Our Creator
A Predetermined Amount of Seconds, Minutes, Hours,
Days, Months, Years, Decades, Life-times
The Blank Page ~is~ Today
A Clear Canvas to Create, Design, Paint, and Author
Live it with Texture
That Feels Your Ability to See the Sun, the Grass, the Sky and the Moon
The Faces of your Parents, Siblings, Children, Cousins and Friends
To Smell Life's Aromas and Fragrances
That Transports Your Deepest Memories Forward
Simultaneously Triggering Us Forward in Time
Igniting Dreams
Heard from Many of our Beloved
And in many Tongues
Emoted Throughout Our Bodies' as Temples

The Reverberation of the Energetic Vibration of the Words
I Love You. . .
Taste the Blessing of our Learned Experiences
Our Bitters and Our Sweets
Moments Lived with Hast Knowing There's Not Time to Waste
With ALL of Our Sensors Finely-Tuned
We are Aware *"The Clock"* is Ticking
Louder with the Passing
Of Each Day ~
The Blank Page
To Take ACTION
To Experience ALL
Of the Things Still Linger Within Our Hearts' Desires
To Step Out from Behind
Make Known to ALL You Love
On This
The Blank Page
Today
I LOVE YOU

Christopher Brooks

Park City

A vast field of asphalt
baking in the sun
surrounds the electric-neon consumer paradise.

Winter, spring, summer, fall,
rain, sleet, snow,
mid-day sun, or gloom of night,
the temperature is constant:
68 degrees fahrenheit,
the lighting bright and unrelenting.

Pubescent girls in ripped jeans
exposing budding pulchritude
stroll past lingerie stores
featuring glossy photographs
of impossibly sexy, nearly naked, women
with painted, pouting, lips.

Balding men in tee shirts
exposing well-fed bellies,
trudge past clothing stores
featuring glossy photographs
of bronzed men with straight, white, teeth,
and impossible musculature.

Christopher Brooks has been a professional violinist his entire life, grew up in Brooklyn; lived in Spain and the Netherlands, currently lives (probably for the rest of his life) in Lancaster, PA. His father was a writer and historian; He grew up in a house filled with books.

Nunzio Caccamo

Exit

A cloud covers the new moon and the shine is gone,
Just like when you finally walked away.

It felt cold that night and it was dark as madness,
Just like when you finally walked away.

I felt the cold wind bruise my face till it was hot and burned,
Just like when you finally walked away.

Today the sun is warm and the breeze is cooling and gentle,
Today is my day to finally walk away.

Nunzio Caccamo is from Olyphant, Pennsylvania. Caccamo was formerly an actor in New York and New Jersey and now takes great interest in poetry and short stories. Caccamo is a member of *Scribblings* writer's club which is currently accepting new members at this link:
https://www.facebook.com/groups/775966783100177

Francesca Creavey

Beach Day in November

Someone drives home in the rain,
with dreams of sleeping longer.
Holding onto something,
anything,
that could make the days go better.

And they long to see the beach,
in the middle of November,
because the weekends are too short
and there is no time in September.

Someone breaks off tiny pieces,
of their mom's vanilla cake.
And they leave it in the alley,
for the ones who eat out too late.

They take just a little time,
to think about what may come tomorrow.
But you can't think about returning
what you still have yet to borrow.

Someone stretches out and yawns,
until they doze off on the couch.
And the world is spinning slower now,
even slower,
until the night has lost all sound.

It's quiet and it's subtle,
and the rain could fall forever.

While somewhere out there,
sleeping soundly,
could be someone's
beach day in November.

Francesca Creavey is a singer and writer from Scranton, Pennsylvania. Her poetry is inspired by the hills and valleys of the Northeast, and all the life that grows in between. Her work was previously featured in the Pennsylvania Bards: Northeast Poetry Review 2020 and Eastern PA Poetry Review 2021.

Abby DeSantis

spare change

he takes shelter in a cardboard box
old newspapers for a bed
threadbare clothes rumpled and dirty
a concrete pillow for his head

picking up used cigarette butts
from the crowded littered street
dumpster diving for table scraps
searching for something to eat

huddling in an open doorway
on a cold cold winter's night
battling to keep warm
swiftly losing the fight

asking hurried passers by
if they have change to spare
no one gives a second look
no one seems to care

a salty tear rolls down
his ruddy weathered cheek
what has happened to his life
that it became so very bleak

Abby DeSantis is a retired fashion executive from New York. Her poems are inspired by nature, hope and the human condition. Abby's poetry has appeared in several anthologies and on-line journals. She currently lives in rural northeastern Pennsylvania with her husband and several furry and feathered friends.

John DeSantis

the last quarter

the last quarter moon looks
like the first in the south
in the half of the earth below
everything seems upside down

the man in the moon at the full
looks like a double you

if you can't travel southward
just invert yourself and you will see
perspective of everything
is made from above
as down is up and up is down

water winds its way down
against the clock as we
in vain attempt to wind
the clock the other way
are in that final quarter too
to try to win in overtime

but do we know that
when the moon is new
again we shall return
again in waking crescent
and will we look left
or will we look right

John DeSantis retired from teaching high school mathematics in the Bronx to a rural life in northeastern Pennsylvania. He has been writing poetry and short stories since early childhood. He is presently at work on two plays and an epivc poem of science fiction. He lives with a dog, three cats and a bird and his wife, Abby, who also writes poetry

Brittany Dulski

The Rookie Cooks Gourmet

It was a cold day in November
With a light dusting of snow
There's a club, my mother's a member
And a meeting to which she must go.

I'd be making the supper tonight,
She had every confidence in me,
It all would be simple as black and white,
As basic as one-two-three.

I'll do it, I'll make tonight's dinner,
So why am I troubled by doubt?
This meal will be a prize winner
My cooking will be a standout.

But the kitchen is a frightful place
With fire and knives and choppers there
It's a scene I'd never face
If I wasn't assigned a meal to prepare.

I'll do it, I'll make tonight's dinner,
So why am I troubled by doubt?
This meal will be a prize-winner
My cooking will be a stand-out.
There's glass that breaks and hot oil that spatters

Machines that grind with an ominous whirr
Dishes that fall with frightening clatters
And mixers that whip with a treacherous purr.

I'll do it, I'll make tonight's dinner,
So why am I troubled by doubt?
This meal will be a prize winner
My cooking will be a stand-out.

No, it's not for me, this cuisine jungle,
I'll settle for frozen microwavable meals
Now, that's something even I can't bungle,
Wait! Is that the smoke alarm's squeal?

Brittany Dulski is from Reading, Pennsylvania. Writing is her major hobby.

Stephanie Evans

Moon Sonnet

Have you seen the nocturnal queen rise up?
She wears a silver gown, and copper crown.
She sips from the Big Dipper, her teacup,
and it brightens her face over our town.
We read romance under her rich mystique
as glossy gloom trails down our moonstone spines.
Are nature's wonders considered antiques?
None fare above her: No ring, nor old wine.
Why does she hang up there, miles away?
She never touches her toes to the waves,
but controls who they kiss and where they sway.
Her light beckons to faraway, dream caves.
       She rises, arabesque, after the sun.
       Her mind at peace, and her heart God has won.

Stephanie Evans lives in Northeastern Pennsylvania. She graduated from Pennsylvania State University, where she studied Business and English. She loves to write fiction and poetry. She is inspired by family, faith, and nature.

Susan L. Peña

Barbie

I picked up that first Barbie at my friend's house,
looked into those sly, painted eyes
and lusted for her.
That bleached updo,
her plastic feet, arched, ready
for those to-die-for high heels.
That knitted black-striped one-piece,
clinging to hard, nippleless breasts.
It was almost too much for my 8-year-old heart.
I wanted that doll.
I wanted the slinky black mermaid dress,
the pink satin prom gown, the works.

But my mother, no fool, knew that girl.
She could see her sneaking a cigarette behind the junior high,
those plastic breasts pressed against the chest
of a leather-clad senior with a Harley.
Mom saw right through those painted eyes.

Later Barbies looked like Sandra Dee,
and went out with that disappointing Ken.
But the first Barbie,
with her dangerous glamour,

made me want to lose the safety
of my childhood, right there and then.

Susan L. Peña is a freelance journalist and writer in Berks County, PA. Since 2020, she has turned to poetry and fiction as well. Her poems have appeared in the PA Bards Eastern PA Poetry Review 2021 and 2023, and in the Schuylkill Valley Journal. She is a member of Berks Bards and hosts their monthly open mic.

Mary C. M. Phillips

small things

the smallest presence
lifts me high
the hummingbird
the lullaby

the pale green bud
announcing spring
the butterfly
the bluebird wing

the star that flickers
in the night
the wisp of cloud
o'er moonlight

the rustle of
the autumn leaves
baby's first step
surely appease

the little things
that bring me low
the turn of head
at a "hello"

the cruel word dropped
in casual time

the short phone call
the quick "goodbye"

the little dog
that is unwell
the chipped teacup
the crackled shell

the smallest things
sway evermore
from mountaintop
to every shore

Mary C. M. Phillips is a caffeinated wife, mother, and writer from the bucolic hills of Lancaster, Pennsylvania. Her spoken-word poetry is available on iTunes and most streaming platforms. She blogs at CaffeineEpipanies.com.

Dean Robbins

Empty Nest

Lying at the edge of the road,
vacant and tilting to one side,
a nest - somehow dislodged, fallen,
discarded from the boughs above.
Emptiness. As if its owners,
having given their children wings
 and encouraged their dreams of flight,
 had decided to move. Someplace
smaller, one floor, and now fewer
rooms. Easier to clean. Nothing
big, and, maybe, not as lonely.

Dean Robbins is 61 years old and lives with his wife, Karen, in Danville, Pennsylvania. He has earned a B.A. and M.A. from Bloomsburg University of Pennsylvania. Robbins has been published numerous times and is a member of the Mill Street Writers in Danville. When neither reading nor writing, he enjoys spending time with his children and grandchildren.

Kimberly Rotter

Insight Requires Utter Imagination

The invisible is much more valuable
to understanding, as obscurity reigns;
Substances which are intangible
is where Reality is contained.

Dark matter is a bizarre material
that won't absorb, reflect, emit energy or light;
Its essence is utter ethereal
yet it protects the cosmos from gravity's might.

This non-baryonic factor
makes up ninety percent of all mass space.
To galaxies it's a great benefactor
keeping them stable spinning at suicide pace.

The universe is pulsating
from an unseen force distributed throughout;
Spread evenly in space and time, agitating,
Dark Energy influence never dilutes or gives out.

Accelerating the expansion rate
of everything over time steadily,
its influence will never abate;
It causes chaos and entropy.

The universe is undetectable
and can't be understood through 5 senses.

Artistic vision makes it accessible
through Imagination, the best insight lens.

Kimberly Rotter is an English professor at Rowan College and Delaware County Community College. She taught high school for over a decade in Philadelphia and New Jersey. Her poetry has been published in the *Pennsylvania Bards East Anthology, The Baron Anthology, and Anthology of Poetry by Young Americans*. She currently lives in The City of Brotherly (and Sisterly) Love with her husband Dominick and pandemic pup Lotte.

George Schaefer

Streetwalker

She was a street walker
by all accounts
She had a plastic rose
pitifully shedding petals
proudly adorned in her hair

But she did have moxie
and an awareness of diners
At her recommendation
I found an old school diner
serving greasy breakfast fair

As it was only fair
and I alone to boot
I invited her to break fast with me
Order what you like
It's all on me

Chatting over coffee
and buttered rye toast
Her sometime sordid
sometime glorious past
poetically brought to life

She hungrily tore into eggs
yet somehow she was lovelier
than most dates I've had

She was certainly kinder
and possibly saner

I had a full docket
but I handed her a Jackson
on the promise of lunch
I really hoped she would
get a good lunch or dinner

She deserved better
than what life threw her way
but carried better grace than most
myself included
I'm not too proud to admit

George Schaefer is a Philly born poet who has been poetically drifting thru life. The verse has been flowing for over 4 decades and the passion for the word continues. He has several volumes available but often forgets to hype them.

J D Shirk

Meadowlands

Grass and weeds grew tall
Nearly shoulder high to the boy
He knew some by name
Milkweed, Shepard's Purse, mint
nettles, and dock
Listed in a borrowed herbarium
A potpourri of July heat, sun
Endless childhood summer days
Cricket song and dragonflies

Sycamores and willows
Meandering shade along the brook
Became the Sherwood Forest
An imaginarium that surely brought a smile
To Howard Pyle, watching from somewhere

Cudgel duels with brambles
"Stand aside thou thorny knave..."
A longbow made of sumac
strung with discarded farmer's twine
Arrows peeled from willow
An archer known throughout
Fair Nottingham

Years have passed, the boy has grown
Now Lord of his Locksley Manor
Married to the fairest maiden

There are grounds to keep,
Gold to earn, faires to attend
Far away from meadowlands and Sherwood

Where grass and weeds grow tall
Beside the road, distant willows call
across the meadowlands
An unseen brook flows
Somewhere through the shaded places

Just for a moment the man pauses
Remembering
Just for a moment, to watch the dragonflies,
To see the willows swaying

Just for a moment there was someone
there, waving from the willows
From Sherwood
It must have been imagination
The meadows had that effect

The man slowly continues on his way
Past milkweeds, mint, and grass
Glancing back from time to time
On the road to Kirklees Priory
Looking back to the meadowlands
Where someone, still was waving

Joe grew up in south eastern Pennsylvania. Raised in an old order Mennonite family. Later, traveling around the nation as a musician developed a deep connection to nature and the sacred in all things.

WISCONSIN

Jan Chronister

Struggling to Put Food on the Table

The Chinese hand-pollinate pears,
wrap each one in a paper sack to protect
fruit from blight.

Blueberry pickers endure
bugs and heat for half a
bucket of indigo globes.

Spearfishers balance
in boats, headlamps
revealing meals
for elders and kin.

Ricers knock kernels
into canoes,
parch, thresh, winnow
manoomin,
"food that grows on the water."

Recently laid off from
six-figure jobs,
unemployed CEOs
are struggling,
newspapers report.

-previously published in *Red Cedar*

Jan Chronister lives in northern Wisconsin. She is part of a network of poets who held a reading to benefit the food shelf in Ashland when the 2018 Wisconsin Bards Against Hunger was published.

Eloisa Gómez

The Round Plate of Poverty

Childhood poverty was not just
the arroz y frijoles that fed
a family of nine
but the many nights in a row
mom served them.

A half-moon of plump textured rice
smelling of garlic and tomatoes
served on round plates
the other semi-circle filled with
refried beans --a dollop of lard already
mashed in.

We'd tear off pieces of tortilla,
Slide it across the plate
the blended half-moons
were eaten quickly.

Poverty just wasn't
the used '60s Hullabaloo boots
with the nifty side zipper,
but the white shoe polish
I painted over dark scuff marks,
hoping classmates believed
they were new.

And it wasn't the hand-me-down

171

First Communion dress I wore
with the one thin ruffle
along the bottom,
but the Cinderella moment I felt
sitting among rows of 8-year old girls
In store-bought, shiny, satineen dresses.

Poverty felt round, not like
the boldness of a full moon
but the feel
of being a spoke in a wheel
rolling down a hill.

Eloisa Gómez is co-author of *Somos Latinas: Voices of Wisconsin Latina Activists* (Wisconsin Historical Society Press, 2018). Much of Eloisa's poetry reflects her experiences living in Milwaukee's central city and includes meditations on poverty, acculturation, and the meaning of familia. Her poem, *Charlie's Coat*, was included in the Bards against Hunger Chapbook – 2018 and *Manuelita La Mariposa* was published in Bramble, Fall 2022. She is a member of the Wisconsin Fellowship of Poets (WFOP) and two local poetry groups.

Heidi C. Hallett

Written in Moss

Rivers of moss
flow over forest hills,
romantic and strong,
finespun, prehistoric.

Mossy rills tell
of glaciers and stories,
ancient Earth
and jungle glory.

Year in, year out,
soft moss streams
in steady, mogul waves—
elegant, jade cascades.

Violet shadow ink
glides as scrolling script,
a wildwood diary
in tidal moss writ.

Heidi C. Hallett sees creative expression through poetry as a way to collaborate and converse. She finds that poetry enables us to examine and appreciate life, and she enjoys working with the imagery in poems to explore ideas. Heidi is a recently retired, small animal veterinarian who paints with oils as well as words, often using these two art forms to complement each other. She is the author of several poetry chapbooks through Local Gems Press, and her poetry has been published in on-line and print journals as well as in numerous print anthologies. www.aquaartideas.com.

Cristina M. R. Norcross

What I Packed for You

We place and stack your new, shiny things
for the dorm in our car.
The clear boxes hold
instant oatmeal and crackers,
because I won't be there
to make you things late at night.
They hold extra shampoo and tissues,
in case you run out of essentials.
They hold a soft robe and new socks,
because this is how my love is translated—
into things you will wear.

Mixed in with the notebooks and highlighters
are stamps and envelopes
for the letters we hope you might write to us,
hooks to hang your favorite poster of wildflowers,
a First Aid kit, because I won't be there
to hand you a Band-Aid
or bring you Advil
when you get your first cold.

Away from home, I will still be with you.
In these clear, overstuffed boxes,
somehow my hands will appear.
You will see what I touched
and touch the love tucked inside,
holding you—still.

Cristina M. R. Norcross lives in Wisconsin and is the editor of *Blue Heron Review*. Author of 9 poetry collections, a multiple Pushcart Prize nominee, and an Eric Hoffer Book Award nominee, her most recent collection is *The Sound of a Collective Pulse* (Kelsay Books, 2021). Cristina's work is featured by the Academy of American Poets (Poets.org). www.cristinanorcross.com

Elizabeth Harmatys Park

abundance

at the convention,
seated in the glittering
grand ballroom awed
by the bountiful banquet
she had to imagine
heaven would be like this
for those who lived
and died hungry

at the country club buffet,
so lavish and well beyond
what the guests could
consume at one meal
she had to go into the kitchen
to ask the serving staff
if they could take home
the leftovers - yes, they could

in the house she knew
as a child there was scarcity
mostly from poverty and
because her mother
didn't like to cook
and didn't like to eat
so her whole life she
marveled at abundance

Elizabeth Harmatys Park is a poet and sociologist. She has received the First Place Jade Ring Poetry Prize awarded by the Wisconsin Writers Association. Her poetry has been published in journals, anthologies and in three chap books.. Park writes with Authors Echo in Burlington, WI and is a regular contributor to the Wisconsin Poetry Calendar.

Sara Sarna

Dear Girl

Dear girl, I say to myself,
though I don't hold myself

dear, and perhaps that's
why I say it now, as if

the hearing of it will inspire
a pause in language

less kind. Dear girl,
don't let disappointments

of your childhood cause
you to set a low bar.

Let go of expectations
born from misguided acquisitions

of others. Make choices,
make mistakes, make amends,

make a life. Whether you have
a thousand minutes or

just one,
there is time.

Sara Sarna is a poet, actor and avid hiker in southeastern Wisconsin where she lives with her husband and crazy rescue dog. Her work has appeared in print and online, been heard on stage and radio and been interpreted by artists in several exibits. Her chapbook, "Whispers from a Bench" was published in 2019.

Jo Scheder

Unsettled, 1976

Backlit by the dusty bus window
her grey head slumped unknowingly
against my stranger's arm

the ancient woman quietly rouses
glances up at my unexpected face
with a silent startle

Maybe she was dreaming of home
Vietnam somewhere, now
who is this auburn-haired [ghost] woman

Quick smiles exchanged with subtle nods
she gazes forward, straightens,
turns to the window

the ocean below,
its vastness compressed
by longing and memory

We are joined by chance in solitary thought
riding along the cliff's edge
up the California coast

Jo Scheder explores poetry as alternative ethnography, following a career as an anthropologist. Her poems appear in *Verse Wisconsin*; *Bramble Literary Magazine*; *Leaves of Peace Anthology*; *Bards Against Hunger 5-Year Anniversary Anthology*; the *Beat Generation Anthology*; and *Poetry Hall Chinese & English Bilingual Journal*. *She lives in Madison, Wisconsin.*

Paula Schulz

Prayer for a common language
for Shuku in her fifth year

She walks beneath the jacaranda trees,
looks up to see the petal-printed sky
warm and mild and welcome as a breeze
in summer's surprising heat. She is wise

for one so small and she is learning how
letters work, their sounds, their shapes like branches
of this tree that writes its story wide. Now
a calling: strange-to-my-ears birdsong launches

itself into air--yet another
language the child and I may learn. Each day
the world speaks in many voices. Brothers,
sisters, each of us has something to say.

We grow as flowering trees, live here under
the same sun, taste the same air.
We can learn how to speak out the wonders
our eyes record, share our stories, share

our lives, brief as tissues, vibrant as blossoms.
written at Tshwane Lutheran Seminary, Pretoria South Africa

Previously Published in Wisconsin Poets' Calendar

Paula Schulz has taught for many years, has recently reached retirement age and lives and writes in Slinger Wisconsin, with her husband, Greg.

Peggy Trojan

Lunch Guest, 1939

Mom, who's that man on the steps?
>Just somebody passing through.

Why is he here?
>Because he was hungry.

What is he eating?
>A fried egg sandwich.

And coffee?
>Yes, and coffee.

Why is he eating out there?
>He said he liked it outdoors.

How did he know where we lived?
>I guess they tell each other.

Where is he going?
>Back to the train, I think.

Is he ever coming back?
>Probably not.

Why did he call you "Ma'am"?
>I think he was just being polite.

Peggy Trojan's new release, a collection about her father, titled *PA*, won second in the Wisconsin Fellowship of Poets Chapbook contest in 2022. She is the author of two full collections and six chapbooks. She lives in Brule, Wisconsin. Her books are available on Amazon.

Susan Schwartz Twiggs

Regrets

I see her clearly,
pale with natural blond hair.
fourteen or fifteen years old.
I am in charge of her,
hired to keep her safe.
I place her in a farm family,
a responsible one.

In my twenties, newly graduated
I wear miniskirts, my favorite—
short brown leather with a string tie.
One afternoon the foster father calls.
He comes to the Cities for business.
"Would you like to meet for dinner?"
I decline. I have no interest.
It's unprofessional.

No one talks about abuse,
about the power imbalance between a girl
and the foster father who houses her.

I wonder what happened to her,
the teenage foster girl.

Fifty years later, I regret—
Why didn't I ask?
Why didn't I ask?

Susan Schwartz Twiggs is inspired by Wisconsin's lakes and Arizona's deserts. She is currently working on a historical novel-in-verse for children. She thanks her critique group, Cabin Fever, for their skillful editing and her husband, John for his continued patience.

Ed Werstein

Loss

Compensating for my hearing loss
I turn on closed-captioning
while watching a mystery movie
and discover a list poem:
lion roars
lion roars again
fanfare music plays
music fades
indistinct chatter
ominous music plays
sirens wail
crowd noises
woman screams
shots fired
footsteps running
screaming continues
door slams
sirens in the distance
dramatic music playing
knocking
door opens
shots fired
a thud
door slams
woman sobbing
footsteps on stairs
siren wails

dramatic music plays
siren fades
music fades
the end

Ed Werstein is a Regional VP of the Wisconsin Fellowship of Poets. In 2018 he received the Lorine Niedecker Prize from the Council for Wisconsin Writers, judged by Nickole Brown. *Communique: Poems From the Headlines* is the latest of his four books of poetry. More at edwerstein.com

INDIANA

Jennifer Criss

Seven Things I Want to Say to My Daughter

1.   You. Are. Beautiful. I don't say this just as your mother. I know I am biased. But people used to stop me on the street to comment on your eyes, your curly hair, your smile, but mostly your big, brown eyes. They'd look at me, then at you, and back to me as if trying to figure out where you came from. You must look like your father. And you do.

2.   You are funny. You crack jokes with a wit that astounds me. You are sarcastic and snarky but very seldom mean-spirited in it. You appreciate a good pun when you hear one and you out dad joke even your Dad.

3.   You are brave. I love how you can stand on a stage and belt out "Heart-Shaped Box," and you're not afraid of the screaming parts. You're not afraid of the bright lights or crowds. You seem comfortable in your skin in a way I don't normally see.

4.   You are brilliant. You can't let your disabilities define you. Don't let them hold you back or bring you down. You can overcome them. Please know that *how* you get there is less important than the fact that you get there. Please stop thinking you're not good enough. You are more than your diagnosis.

5.   You. Are. Loved. I know you feel alone so much and that no one can possibly understand what it's like to be you. You retreat from the world, buried in your blankets, and feel worthless. You don't see your place. But I have loved you fiercely from the moment I knew you existed and have never stopped.

6.   You are needed. I need you to try to pull back from that darkness that surrounds you like a dense fog. I can't imagine a world without you in it, and I don't want to. There would be an unfillable hole left in the fabric of the universe were you not here. I need you on this planet!

191

7.   You. Are. Beautiful. I don't say this as just your mother. From your perfectly winged eyeliner to the black lipstick- from your peach/pink hair to your floral-meets-leather- "I don't care" - style. You are beautiful, but it's mostly your heart. You have a beautiful, funny, brave, brilliant, lovely heart that can fight through all this seemingly impossible murk. And I need you to know this.

Jennifer Criss is a content strategist and writer for Ball State University. She is currently pursuing a master's in emerging media, design, and development. Her work has been published in *Poebita, Whispers, The Poet Community, Indiana Voice Journal,* and several print anthologies. She was nominated for a Pushcart Prize in 2016 and released her own tiny book of poetry in 2019 titled *When You Tell Me to Smile.*

Joseph Pete

The War that Followed us Home

A few of us died in the war.
We got shot, nicked surgically by shrapnel to the carotid artery, torn clear limb from limb
in profligate splatter they'd mop up like muddy boot tracks
while grabbing creamed corn and rubbery chicken in a cafeteria line at the FOB,
where they served the purported heroes the same lowest-bidder slop they fed to convicts.

Many more of us died after returning home
to the comfort of hot showers and fluorescently lit grocery superstore aisles.
We overdosed on heroin, drowned in swimming pools,
wrecked our glistening new motorcycles on scenic highways on the California coastline.

We left the war with our overstuffed duffel bags, sweat-soaked camo, and storage conexes.
But the war never left us behind.
It followed us back home to the land of body wash, air conditioning, and plush mattresses,
a place of comfort where you could safely grab a moment's rest.
We thought we came back to a new chapter, a fresh beginning,
but the war never really left us at all.

Sure, it swapped locales and changed scenery,
but the war rebooted and reinvented itself in a reborn host.
After all those years, the war stayed in the same place,

right in the dead center of our deadened, aching, throbbing skulls,
in the neurons firing back-and-forth in a senseless and rampant cacophony.

Joseph S. Pete is an award-winning journalist, author, veteran, Society of Professional Journalists board member and Pushcart Prize nominee who frequently appears on Lakeshore Public Radio. His literary work has appeared in more than 100 journals, including Prairie Winds, Gravel, Chicago Literati, The Offbeat, Perch Magazine, and Tipton Poetry Journal. Like Bartleby, he would prefer not to.

Teresa Pruitt

The shanty

Visible from just one look
 the foundation had been shook.
The winds had fiercely blown through,
ravishly breaking a few
 parts and pieces as it shook.

Leaving fragile window panes
with rain they could not contain,
with their crowded, countless, cracks
and their panes absent of glass,
they enabled torrent rains.

Times' devoted, ruthless role
had apprehended lives' toll.
That bloodthirsty curse of time
to lives' veins had been unkind,
destruction leaving a hole.

The blows from the savage storm
gave life to an altered form,
a crumbling, shattered new face,
desolations' new home place,
delicate, tragic, reform.

As life stormed out of control,
destruction took its slow stroll,
making a majestic mess.

The wreckage that was endless,
formed the shanty of my soul.

Teresa Pruitt was born and raised in Indiana. She is a retired mother of 5 and grandmother to 15. After retirement, she took up writing as one of her many hobbies. She has entered and placed in the local Poetry society of Indiana competitions.

Stacy Savage

Through a Poet's Eyes

She sees a spider
With more beats to her heart.
The poet sees a weaver
Who creates works of art.

He dismisses the cardinal
In winter's beams of light,
But the poet sees the scarlet
Enhancing all the white.

She sees the moonlight
As the ending of a day
But the poet sees the diamonds
As fireflies light the way.

He sees a mighty oak
As only just a tree,
But the poet sees a witness
Of so much history.

He sees the meadow
As just an empty space,
But the poet sees the deer
Among buttercups and lace.

She sees the caterpillar
As just an ugly thing,

But the poet sees beauty
That will soon spread its wings.

Within the eyes of wordsmiths
Reflects nature's worth,
But all of us can appreciate
The jewels of Mother Earth.

-First published in Sequoia Cherokee River Journal, issue 7, 2020

Stacy Savage has published several anthologies that benefited multiple char-
ities. Her work has been published in numerous publications, including Birds
and Blooms, Ideals magazine, Asian Geographic, and Tipton Poetry Journal.
She was a judge twice in the former Best Books of Indiana competition that
was held by the Indiana State Library. She's currently working on a mental
health project that she expects to be published in Spring 2023.

NEW JERSEY

Radhika Baruah

A Love Song in the Rain

You did not look back, rain
Drenched my skies: every inch
With vision watering into a
Blurr, I watched hibiscus bloom

In shades of tangerine.
I grew into a tangent before
My very eyes; a silent spectator
Waiting. You kept up your pace

Walking, never once looking back
Your footsteps fell heavily; yet erased
Instantaneously in puddles, leaving
Gaping wounds- like rose buds

Stuck among ivy, choking
Unable to survive the onslaught
You walked away; my life
Walked away too

Locked inside your coat pockets.

Radhika Baruah, a bilingual freelance educator, hails from Assam, India. She has lived in several cities and is currently based in New Jersey, USA. She finds writing and translating a therapeutic hobby. Her work has appeared in several newspapers, magazines and anthologies including The Assam Tribune, MuseIndia, Chay Magazine, Fried Eye, Haiku Journal, New Jersey Bards Central Poetry Review 2020, and The 50-Word Stories of 2021.

Tabitha Dial

Half Full

They are going bad.
I don't know if I'll have to throw away
half a box of strawberries

because I can't seem
to eat them fast enough
or because it is predetermined:
I only will eat so many

but--
Law of Strawberry or nature of time--
they don't taste half so good without you.

Tabitha Dial wants you to create your fate. She won the Penned Literary Contest with her poem "Green Soup" and published her first book, "Creative Divination: Read Tea Leaves and Develop your Personal Code". She works as a substitute teacher and lives in Plainsboro, New Jersey. Social media and Tarot and Tea Leaf Readings available from Tabitha at NorthStarMuse.com

Lynette G. Esposito

In My Dead Mother's House

I keep looking above the refrigerator
Where my mother kept her yellow octagon shaped clock
For the time

It hasn't been there for many years,
Yet,
When I want to know the hour,
I look there
As if things stay the same, as if
Certain points and places do not change,
As if she were still alive
giving advice and criticism.

Strange snakes slither through
The mind making amends for little guilty
Transgressions, swallow memories,
Eat names of friends and cousins, strangle
Thought,
Expose a stark clarity to reality.

I look inward and see the past replayed
with vivid lucidity in present time.

Yet.
When I want to know the time,
I look at an empty wall.

Lynette G. Esposito, MA Rutgers, has been published in Reader's Digest, Poetry Quarterly, North of Oxford, Remembered Arts, Twin Decades, Fox Chase Review, Deep Overstock and others. She was married to Attilio Esposito and lives in Southern New Jersey with eght bossy feline muses

Beulah Gordon-Skinner

On Autumn

The trees are naked;
Branches devoid of sated rows
of acorns, pecans, apples and pears

Leaves strewn onto fields-
faded hues of browns,
burnt oranges and yellows

Wrestled by the wind.
Timberland.

Poet and Lyricist Beulah Gordon-Skinner is a writer member of the American Society of Composers, Authors & Publishers (ASCAP). Originally from Elizabeth City, North Carolina, she currently resides in Pennsauken, New Jersey.

Jamie Hardges

HE walks me through

Living my life
struggling to walk with GOD
traveling a road that's never been trod
wading through troublesome waters
hands bound together with iron clad fetters
shoulders slumped over like a withering flower
the enemy laughs at my tears
mocks me
calls me a coward
i close my eyes so tight
and inhale a puff of air
i put MY mind on MY GOD
i walk in faith
I KNOW HE CARES!
i know with GOD on my side
i have NOTHING to fear
my weeping eyes are DRY now,
because HE'S wiped EVERY TEAR!
I'm free!
and now i see
the light
a path so clear
i pick myself up
i lift my head high
i walk with my father
i now have NEW life
we soar to new heights

we take a road thats never been seen
fluffy clouds
we bathe in the warm sun
the luscious grass
so smooth,
so green
a fragrant flowery scent
marks this moment in time
i have no worries
no cares
i hold my saviours hand in mine
i kiss the sky
GODS love kisses me back
lets me know HE'LL carry me through
with a love so dear
so true
HE'll never turn HIS back
when i feel i cant make it
HE'LL be there to pick up the slack
this love anew, genuine, refreshing
so crisp, so cool
its a breeze
i'm on my knees
thanking GOD for catching me
every time i fall
HE answers MY call
and lifts me high
i'm the apple of his eye
i couldnt imagine, never ever dream
how this mess in a dress
that was helpless
could stand before you now FREE!
I DECLARE IT!

I have new life!
I am now made brand new
and i owe GOD a huge debt of gratitude
for without HIM i'd still be on that endless road
wandering,
spinning,
in circles
confused...
and without a clue!

Janet Lee

Embeddedness
for Becky

When I see a lily in the garden,
I see the overlapping petals
sliding like shoji screens
in the shifting morning air -
creating swaths of colors so subtle
they have yet to be named.

I see the buds,
the tight geometric bundles
whose only job
is to burst open.

I see the nut hard seeds.

When I see you,
I see my early marriage,
my new motherhood,
and my first born.

You are the nut, the bud, and the bloom.

When I see you,
I see our first apartment in Chinatown,
the crib in the living room,
and your striving to learn everything at once.

Now you live in a city bathed in fog, and
I am the nut, the bud, and the bloom.
But I am no longer in the garden -
you will have to come and find me.

Janet Lee is a writer and social worker from New Jersey who works with survivors of domestic violence helping them find safety and healing. She finds storytelling and poetry a part of that healing, for both survivors of trauma and those who seek to help them.

Shelagh Naughton

Racoon's Rant

'T was in the middle of the night when Eva got an awful fright
For in the middle of her stairs she glimpsed a cheeky raccoon there
"Oh Eva dear you're up so late" the raccoon stated (it was one of her traits)
To speak directly with human words but Eva thought it quite absurd
A talking raccoon upon her stair invading her house without a care
She tried to breathe deeply, keep her fear at bay, attempted to stop her legs giving way
She pursed her lips to stop herself wailing and clung on to her wooden railing
She took a deep breath and managed to say, "Mrs Raccoon how are you to-day?"
Eva couldn't believe those words came out but was trying to reason what this scene was about
Mrs Raccoon noticed her angst ridden face and reassured Eva with her animal grace
"I know it's not the norm for you to see a raccoon speaking just like me"
But one day I woke up and had a human voice so you see I didn't really have a choice
It's not my intent to instill fear and strife but now as you see this is my life
And now I do have a voice, I have much to say. To all you humans I would like to convey
Our objections to comments you share each day on our lifestyles and our raccoon ways
The label, "Scavengers" you humans call us really does offend and appall us
Just for rustling our hearty fare from the garbage cans you leave out there
We don't have supermarkets with food in to buy, no metal pans for our meals to fry
It's work and effort to get our food, no array of delights to suit our mood

211

And just because my little kits, my girls and boys, happen to make a little noise

Doesn't mean you chase them in the street before their bellies have something to eat

I think if you are throwing food scraps away (without the objections) we'll eat them that day

We'll collect it at night as we usually do but without the drama from other humans like you

If you could share these requests Eva, with your human friends, we could start to make amends

We can live cohesively tomorrow and all the other days to follow

We'll collect our scraps as quietly as can be and we'll all get along fairly happily

Eva was slightly overwhelmed by her onerous task although she understood Mrs Raccoon's ask

She wasn't sure how to spread the news of a talking raccoon with opinions and views

She feared her mental state would be questioned if she shared her chat with the   aforementioned

A talking raccoon? She could hear them all reply. The shame of sharing it, she would want to die

Of the embarrassment and ridicule sure to follow but she knew that she couldn't fret and wallow

So she asked Mrs Raccoon if she would agree to meet all her human friends that lived on her street

Well Mrs Raccoon considered for a while, celebrity raccoon was not really her style

But eventually after Eva pressed Mrs Raccoon did acquiesce

An organized meeting took place in the hood. The humans listened the raccoons were understood

No documents hidden, no raccoon space raided, no raccoon or human feeling tired and jaded

A healthy discussion had taken place, no insults flew from anyone's face

No master needed to oversee the proceedings, no copious amounts of legal meetings
A talking raccoon had aired her views and no one on the street had shouted "FAKE NEWS!!"

Shelagh Naughton is a teacher and music specialist in New York City. She writes original children's songs and wrote and co-produced her C.D; City Songs, 'A School Year In The Big Apple' in 2016. She lives in New Jersey, USA.

Tom Pawlowski

Contentment

Sitting beside you
Comforted by your breathing
Steady and relaxed

Fashion Sense

I think that buttons
Could learn a lesson from you
About being cute

Chiaro di luna

Moon shines through window
Allowing just enough light
To reveal your charms

Tom Pawlowski (tomp) is a life-long resident of South Jersey. In 2012 he made a New Year's resolution to write a haiku everyday, and he hasn't stopped yet. He has previously been published in *"Tea-ku"*, *"Twin Towers, Twin Decades"*, *"Beat Generation"*, *"Chaos - Poetry Vortex"* (all 2021); *"Trees in a Garden of Ashes"* (2020); *"NJ Bards South Poetry Review"* and *"Bards Against Hunger - New Jersey"* (both 2019) and participated in *"Pitman Poems on Parade"* from 2015 through 2018.

Megha Sood

Ingredients for Happiness

They say, kindness comes from the heart
But hunger pierces a man the most
My mother always said,
So learn to soothe that hunger
those incessant wanting,
those innumerable desires.

Those that sit precariously between the soft folds of our soul
That jagged hunger that only can be satiated
by those deft supple wrinkled hands
coated with the flour and oil
kneading the dough in the warm summer afternoon
soaked by the apricity of the sun.

What is the definition of happiness?
There are many yet none.

A belly stuffed with the desire
to be fed an ambrosial meal by the loved ones
A lingering need that clings to
our soft parts thick as greed
waiting to grow,
wanting to heal.

Those moments pitted with joy,
Those moments pregnant
with the proximity of the loved ones

brimming with passion
soaked with the unending desires
acts like a tourniquet for our bleeding self.

As we gather around the whistling teapot
surrounded by the verdant greens of the *Gaia*
embellished with the soft pockets of clouds
floating carelessly on a warm summer afternoon
suffused with healing and nostalgia in equal measures

Those precious moments
when the air is suffused with the aroma
of warm freshly cooked home meal
douse the desires in your belly
and syncopates with the mellifluous melody
of the long-lost tunes.

What more could a heart want?

Than to be around the kitchen table
a sole witness of our contentment and wanting;
for times unknown,
Where every grain of the wood is ingrained
with the little joys and nostalgia of life
lived to the brim
stripped of its loneliness,
brimming with unmeasurable elation

Of being together as one family
kneaded like a lump of dough
as a dollop of the milky white moon;

Waiting to rise
out of warmth,
Together.

Megha Sood is an Award-winning Asian American Poet, Editor, Author, and Literary Activist from New Jersey, USA. Recipient of 2021 Poet Fellowship from MVICW (*Martha's Vineyard Institute of Creating Writing)* and a National Level Winner for the *2020 Poetry Matters Project*. Recipient of *"Certificate of Excellence"* from Mayor, Jersey City. Associate Poetry Editor Literary Journals *Mookychick(UK)*, *Life and Legends (USA)*, and Literary Partner with *"Life in Quarantine"*, Stanford University. Author of Chapbook (*"My Body is Not an Apology"*, Finishing Line Press, 2021) and Full Length (*"My Body Lives Like a Threat"*, FlowerSongPress,2021). She blogs at https://meghasworldsite.wordpress.com/ and tweets at @meghasood16.

DELAWARE

Lisa G. Black

1212

Late nights, early mornings
but never did I see the warning

long drive talks,
deck dinners,
beach walks

steadfast with sound advice,
humor was our device
fifty plus years does not suffice

reluctantly, we now are mourning
And never did I see the warning

Ms. Black is a seasoned award-wining film producer and creative manager. As Founder and President, she successfully runs her company Garnet Girl in support of creatives globally. With an early passion for artistic expression; Lisa's first poem was penned at age seven. Her poetry style is a journalistic expression of relationships encountered along her travels. Twice included in the Delaware Bards poetry review she resides northern Delaware, with her husband raised two children and is a citizen of the world.

Lyndsey Collison

Be That Kid

Always be that kid
That stands up for the weak
Always be that kid

That seeks the highest peak

Always be that kid
That is full of love
Always be that kid
That rises above

Always be that kid
That stands tall in self pride
Always be that kid
That stands by her friends side

Just always be that kid
That makes her family proud
Remember you are that kid
Where uniqueness is your sound

Savanna Evans

knots

a woman lays in bed
its an hour after noon
the sun threatens to pierce through her curtains
and her hair is full of knots

a young man wonders in the morning
dreaming of words he's yet to say
anxious and ever so peaceful
and his stomach is full of knots

she dreamt that night of his presence
his soul intertwined with hers
she dreamt of rest and of safety
and her heart is full of knots

he aches for her to enter his arms again
it's been a month, where to begin
is her heart one he could win?
and his mind is tied up in knots

every loop and twist they take
every silent thought and ache
every tangle, each mistake
becomes a web of love they make

savanna evans is young and learning how to grow into who she is. she lives on the edge of womanhood and eagerly places those feelings on pen and paper, which she calls good friends. she is thrilled to call you a reader.

Sarah Gordon

The Ocean is Calling

The ocean is calling on this hot, summer day
My heart filled with excitement - opportunities to play

The sky is vivid blue with elegant, white clouds
Waves hitting the shoreline, creating a stirring sound

It is a perfect day, in almost every single way
Time spent enjoying and relaxing...a day just slipping away

How is it possible to stay in such bliss for so long?
And to somehow memorize it all like a beautiful love song

Should I be content for this one day in time?
And learn from its magic to help others begin to shine

The ocean is calling on this hot, summer day
As I walk towards it slowly, in my own, unique way

Making joyful memories, living life, not much more to say
It feels all so simple, and yet, surely God's work is on display

As I dream with excitement for a time to come back
For now, I will smile at such beauty and just reflect

The ocean is calling as I lose all sense of time by the hour
With the sweet smell of sea mist, the movement, the power

As I look back once more, for a glance at the day's past
The sun begins to soften, and shadows start to cast

For I entered the ocean on this day with childlike glee
And I left as an adult, my heart overflowing and free

It was an extraordinary day, a gift, a reminder to just be
I hope to be back one day to embrace you, my friend - the sea

Sarah Gordon enjoys life along the Eastern Shores of Delaware in a small beach community called Bethany Beach. She is a full-time student working on her doctorate in Health and Human Performance. When not studying, she spends time on the beautiful nature trails and coastal water settings, both of which inspire her poetry.

John Grau

Dream Girl

You came to me last night – long time, this time.
I dreamed I was in my dream kitchen;
white hand-painted tile and maple woodwork gleaming
in sunlight streaming through vaulted ceiling skylights.
Chatting with workmen, still finishing up,
bustling about the marble counters
and handsome cabinets, some tool slipped
breaking the set of canisters bought years ago
on honeymoon in Belize. I went to tell my wife,
tapping her on the butt as she stretched across
the island reaching for God knows what.
And *you* turned around:
forty-something yet still possessing
that girlish allure of my mind's eye;
 jeans and powder-blue blouse, your favorite color;
hair plain and short, brushed back,
as always, behind your ears.
And most of all, glowing.
You smiled brightly, whispering something
I could not make out and followed with a kiss
that said whatever I had to tell could wait.

How many times have you,
out-of-the-blue, burst to mind,
co-opting attention, seizing emotion?
Two frightened young lovers
in a New York City clinic; your distress

beamed into the waiting room,
blotting thought, stopping time.
Ironic that, in the end, we could never find
wave lengths on much else that mattered.

Even after parting, you would come
unexpected, unbidden;
my thoughts restless and brooding.
Then some news.

The time I trudged around for months unable
to stop thinking about you and then,
by chance, hearing from an old friend
that you had gotten married.
Or, years later, after staggering
through weeks in a fog, I knowingly opened
the seldom-read alumni magazine
that had just arrived to find a blurb
that you were teaching in Texas,
the mother of two young children.

But why, after so many years,
should you now come back,
this time in mid night?
This time bringing the joy and abandon
of the night we placed a fragile patch
over our broken engagement
and made love until dawn?

What news?
Some fortune, some tragedy
once again lighting up our emotional hotline?
What was it you whispered?

Was it farewell?
That all has worked out
as happily for you
as it had for me?

What news?
Or was this just some random
hello-goodbye of two people who,
once "connected," can never unplug?
Or perhaps merely another
in the long parade of phantoms
of the night, stirred by a chance turn
onto some overgrown memory lane?

What news?
What message could possibly matter
on the other end of long lives
we've made with others?
Lives of untold joys and heartbreaks
transforming us into people
who would not now recognize
each other if we crossed
paths at an airport or a mall?

Yet, still I ask:
What news?
What news?

John Grau is a retired journalist living in Sussex County, Delaware. His poems have appeared in anthologies in Delaware and the Finger Lakes region of New York, where he lived for 37 years. He is a contributor to Sense of Decency (senseofdecency.com), a blog dedicated to free and respectful discussion of contemporary life in a society torn apart by pandemic and partisanship.

Lily Hearn

Envy

She is a forest fire,
Unable to be tamed, unable to be contained
Carelessly growing, born from a collusion of elements

And I feel I am just the dancing flame
of a candle,
Never too unruly,
And able to be blown out by a passerby's quick breath out. Or a gentle wind.
A sigh can falter me.
But I'll be ignited again
When I'm needed or wanted for comfort in the day or assurance in the dark

But she is a forest fire.
Ravaging life,
Taking life,
Moving in, so terrifyingly,

And I am just the smallest light
She is hated, and I am loved
But she still grows.
And I am over when I'm alone.
Or when the night has come.
She goes on, whether under sun or moon,
Burning brightly and wildly like Hell's monsoon

We both share the same light,
But I am so envious of her might.

229

Lily Sophia Hearn is a writer from Laurel, Delaware. Her work is inspired by her own life experiences, nature, and human instinct and she primarily writes poetry and fiction. She hopes to have more of her work published some day.

Norton Nearly

American Dream

do the homeless dream of two weeks away
escape from their every day-to-day
dream of a change of pace
a visit to a more appealing place
dream of dining on a new cuisine
as seen in a photo in the gutter's magazine
dream of new bought shorts to replace borrowed pants
collecting cans instead of collecting cant's
or are dreams restricted to those in homes
those unfamiliar with hunger-pain moans
are dreams even allowed if one has no hope
worth imagining if one can barely cope
and what are dreams anyway
but useless optimism that runs away

dreams unmade
never fade

let's dream that all may dream
hope for the hope that all deserve to feel

easy for me to dream this dream I guess
under my leakless place of easy rest

Norton Nearly has self published four books which include two volumes of free-verse poetry. Norton is also a "forest artist" who crafts walking sticks and other items out of wood. You can see his work at nortonnearly.com.

Dianne Roberta Scott

Leaving Our Good Story

We are conceived to be born and then born to live; the length of our time is a mystery.

Though while alive for short or long, what our days unfold, the purpose we serve and the life we lead will tell a story.

Since it's unknown when our tale will end, working diligently to fill our pages with good works is most essential.

Why? Because our book will be read, and as the author we'd want to leave those left to mourn an account that's nothing less than special.

Dianne Scott, born and raised in Milford, De has resided in Dover, De for 30 years. She is the proud mother of two (Justin & Jessica) and became a free-lance writer after medically retiring several years ago due to MS progression. In addition to a plethora of articles, she has been published in two anthologies and nearing the completion of her memoir, Sunny With A Chance Of MS.

Johnny M. Tucker, Jr

In a State of Poverty

A blade of grass
limp and tired
stranded on a dry
summer's day
awaits
a-long-time-coming
the very least
a single drop of rain.

A poet, sitting on the curb,
plucks it from its roots and
then blindly tosses it aside—
his soul famished.

From where he sits
watches his own hand
brush atop that same
rough patch of grass,
all the while awaiting
a single verse, a syllable
rich in sound.

Johnny M. Tucker, Jr. is a poet and anthologist. He currently lives in Green-ville, Delaware (United States). To learn more, you can view his website at johnnytuckerjr.com or email him at johnny.m.tucker.jr@gmail.com.

Janet Williams

From The Madness

Take me from this madness
to a place that's nice and green
take me past the beggars waltz
through this cardboard neon scene

Spill the sadness in the streets
watch it spread like sand
take me to the other side
just tell me that I can

Tell me not to paint in blue
you know it fades too soon
but it's hard to see the colors
while living in this gloom

I just watched the sun rise
it's completely lost the light
you know that it's all over
when the day becomes the night

Look for the beauty in the stars
they seem so close to touch
but you know how the stars are
you know they cost too much

Look at the painting on the wall
you feel it's lost and gone

a creative time that was beyond
the sky, the clouds, at dawn

If I could only reach that point
I could throw this all away
and I could be what I once was
but that was yesterday

Janet Williams grew up in Arden, Delaware. She studied fine art, graphic design and wrote poetry. She attended PAFA, graduated from the University of Delaware and Philadelphia University. While living in Philadelphia she had a poem published in the Chestnut Hill local and in 2022 and 2023, she was published in The Delaware Bards Poetry Review. Poetry to her is Art- work painted in words.

MARYLAND

J. Joy "Sistah Joy" Matthews Alford

Haiku #365 – *A Hunger Trilogy*

Some doctors convince
Seniors that their meds not their
Food keeps them healthy

Ms. Jacobsen bought
Each new pill her doctor sold
Trying to get well

Her garden-grown fruit
Rotted on the vine as she
Filed for bankruptcy

J. Joy "Sistah Joy" Matthews Alford is the Inaugural Poet Laureate of Prince George's County, Maryland, and has authored three collections of poetry. She has hosted and produced the nationally recognized poetry cable television program, *Sojourn with Words*, since its inception in 2005, and has served as president of the Poetry Ministry of Ebenezer A.M.E. Church in Fort Washington, Maryland since 2003. She is the founder of Collective Voices, an ensemble of native Washington, DC poets known for their poems of social consciousness, empowerment, and spirituality. She lives in Prince George's County, Maryland.

Alan Barysh

All You Can Eat

They put bleach on the discarded food in the dumpster behind the
All You Can East Buffett
To keep the homeless from taking it
Inside people make food mountains
Only to throw food away they thought they might like to eat
As the steak sauce is slathered on the steak
The whipped cream ladled on the pudding
And soda is guzzled by the gallon
A family is dividing up a slice of pizza so that everyone can get a bite

Alan Barysh is a local Baltimore Activist who was the Maryland Institute Poet
In Residence for the year 2000. He is the author of over one hundred books
on sale at Amazon .Com

Maggie D Brace

Embracing Medusa

Sinuous ebb and flow of medusa's tentacles
mimic the movement of sea grass.
Brainless, carnivorous, consumer.

Newly hatched sea slug devoured in haste,
indigestible shell becomes enmeshed.
Insatiable, vestigial parasite.

Snail attaches, snacks and grows,
within the unsuspecting jellyfish.
Symbiotic, self-preservation.

As nudibranch matures, medusa slowly deconstructs,
bite by bite, meal by meal.
Unique, primordial battle.

Their relationship till death do them part,
Consumed becomes consumer.
Seeking natural order.

We see ourselves a unique property of nature,
Maintaining our own individuality.
Ego begets identity.

Each interaction foments the snails we imbibe,
letting them grow and fester inside.
Consumed, bleakly joyless.

Life goal is to embrace the selfness of us,
and the themness of them.
Copacetic, blissful unity.

Maggie D Brace, a life-long denizen of Maryland, teacher, gardener, basketball player and author attended St. Mary's College and has written *'Tis Himself: The Tale of Finn MacCool* and *Grammy's Glasses*, and has multiple short works and poems and art in various anthologies.

Michael Haldas

The Strange Gift

It's a special gift she told me.
Make sure you treat it with great care.
Endure it with love patiently.
Most people will not understand.
You'll feel like you're going nowhere,
like you're cycling endlessly;
living between hope and despair;
but holding a soul in your hand.

I hung up the phone angrily,
and I walked to the other room.
Her words echoed repeatedly.
How could anyone understand?
A gift! This was more like doom.
It bordered on insanity.
I paced and then started to fume,
yet I had to meet this demand.

Gifts were for Christmas Day morning,
birthdays and special occasions.
From the one you are adoring,
presents that make hearts feel light;
not this type of an invasion;
that made you feel more like mourning.
Despite her heartfelt persuasion,
this gift just couldn't be all right.

I walked outside in frustration,
wanting to forget her strange words.
Fuming in deep consternation,
when a gentle breeze suddenly blew.
A recollection long deferred,
carrying deep revelation;
recalling memory interred,
with sudden clarity I knew.

The memory of my father,
whose death was a sudden surprise.
Shock made me inwardly holler.
We spoke only hours ago,
but soon after came his demise.
Leaving the world without bother,
left us without saying goodbyes.
Causing deep grief that would follow.

One unusually hot spring day,
We finally cleaned the house out.
Exhausted in every way,
a cold wind blew in from the outside.
It erased my pain and my doubt.
Without words I became okay.
I knew what the Wind was about.
My grief now began to subside.

The Spirit was gracing that breeze.
It so refreshed my burdened soul.
Beyond just a strong sense of ease,
it transformed my great suffering
The wounds in my heart became whole.
Grateful I prayed thanks from my knees.

And for months I would extol,
the truth I was discovering.

But from my mind truth gets driven,
because I too often forget
The grace in life I've been given,
that I fail to appreciate.
Realization brings deep regret.
I wish I had better striven,
and not be angry when beset,
when things make my life deviate.

Now this burden was upon me,
deep suffering of another
I thought this was all behind me.
How much more pain could I take?
To avoid it were my druthers,
and I struggled internally
seek happiness said all the others.
A deeper choice I had to make.

This special gift of suffering,
yields a capacity to love
Difficult and so puzzling.
Pushes you to a painful place.
Beyond what your capable of.
The process gives a great humbling,
that can only come from above
Gifting supernatural grace.

Accepting the gift looked so strange,
to many who just didn't know
That the world likes to rearrange,

the truth to preserve its blindness.
We can deeply wish it weren't so.
Others can think we're deranged,
but the truth is it makes us grow.
Selfishness yielding to kindness.

Suffering brought out my best trait,
when I had little to offer.
Always wishing it would abate,
by grace I was illumined.
Though some played the role of scoffer,
thinking I was going to break.
Through grace I had more to proffer,
and it would make me more human.

Suffering is a cross to bear.
It's the strangest gift we receive.
It enables others to share,
from their soul's deepest reservoir.
Though we may want a reprieve.
Deep down we become so aware.
It is not something we should grieve.
We become better than we are.

Michael Haldas is an author, educator, and speaker. His published works include books (non-fiction and fiction), short stories, articles, and poems. He also has a long running podcast show and teaches online adult religious education classes. Visit www.michaelhaldas.com to learn more about his work.

Kaiti Ilana

Surrendering

Sorrows, sweet sadness,
Soak, seep and stain sheets -
Silks of slumber.
Sounds of sorries shriek.
Such scandal through spectating sills?
No single soul stops or stares.
Silent in seeming solitude.
Sacred spaces shattered.
Succeeding seconds smear.
Sentiments of sureness surround.
Sinking, slipping, seeking
Safety in sleep.

Kaiti Ilana is a poet, educator, and creative residing in the farmlands and hillsides of western Maryland. She has been recently published in *Maryland Bards Poetry Review 2022*.

Jane Leibowitz

#1
I wish I could be
a manatee munching on
hyacinth all day.

#2
Unrelenting weeds,
marvelously resilient.
To a fault, I think.

#3
Magnificent green
zucchini leaves turned sodden.
Damn rapacious bugs!

Jane Leibowitz lives on the eastern shore of Maryland, taking inspiration from the countryside and the sea. Writing, painting and cooking are the fruits of her creative labors. She is currently working on illustrating her book of original haiku.

Angelo Letizia

We sat on your porch
In North Carolina
We drank beer
And looked at the stars
I told you
The light takes billions of years
To reach the earth
But the star is dead
This was before our marriage
Before kids and the PhD
Before I thought I knew everything
But the light is still trying to come to earth
And the star is still dead

Angelo Letizia lives in Maryland with his wife and children. He has published
three books of poetry with Silverbow press.

Louis Petrich

He's This, She's That

Can he be rhymed off straight from facts—writ pat?
In love with seas, wet skin, bright curls, green isles.
"I have love for you, friend," she waves, "that's it."
As clouds paint skies, her evanescent smiles
subscribe words lit from distant hands, stealth lips,
for don't bit stars do infinite of black?
Her missives vibrate (not enough) with sips
of overtures that salve somewhat heart's rack
and spur his plenty done more jointed years.
Not fooled enough, sore spent, comes fate grotesque,
for schooled she goes in art of raising cheers,
girl-curious t'anoint boys amouresque.
He might as well be spinning silk to straw:
imagination cleaves to jewels that claw.

Can she be rhymed off straight from facts, bare-boned?
Her friend, long-haired . . . long-tamed . . . with dog she sleeps.
Yet love dared pick him and pertains, phone-laired.
(Her dog would like him more, licked treat to treat.)
Legs chickening, fingers satiate, spell out
fools' fated fallings in across hearts' hacked
divide. How quaint quill perkings punt all doubt
of cursive character: *see! couplings blacked*
unstop her soundings, scored not his who fears!
Her yearnings, teasing turnings, timings tasked
apply to dust equipage pleasing mirrors

(spite shoulders bent) to bluff dusk youthful masked:
"These studs I arm, life's flash to steal!" she pings.
Imagination husbands lying things.

Louis Petrich, originally from Chicago, Illinois, has been a tutor at St. John's College in Annapolis, Maryland for twenty years. He has also taught American studies for a decade in post-communist Romania, Czechoslovakia, and Kyrgyzstan, and biology and mathematics in Kurdish Iraq. He likes to dive the Caribbean island of Bonaire, where he practices underwater photography. He has lectured and published on Shakespeare and Chekhov, whose arts of theater, poetry, and fiction he most attends. He is married and has two children, both students of St. John's.

Matthew Powell

April 14, 1912

I remember the last time
just like it was yesterday
the last time we had dinner
I slid a ring on your finger
as we shared a bottle of wine

the last time I took your hand
your eyes locked on mine
during a long, slow dance

I escorted you to our room
my fingers caressing your body
as you held it against mine

the last time we made love
the taste of your warm lips
your head was on my shoulder
you fell asleep in my arms

then came the terror!
a deafening crash!
as though the whole world
was shaking!
as if Heaven and Hell
were having a final battle
and we were caught in the middle

I tried so hard to save you
held onto you will all my might
but the frigid water rushed in so fast!
there was no escape
we were going down

this is it!
we are going to die
if they ever find the wreckage
I hope they know
our love was true to the end
that I tried
but could not save you
that we died together, holding tight

from my shivering lips
I said
"I love you"
for the last time

Matt is a Maryland resident who's journey in poetry began when he would write "songs" as a teenager. He still writes, not only as a form of therapy, but also as a means to let readers know that they are not alone in their struggles. He has been published in several anthologies by Local Gems Press. He is currently working on his own book of poetry, which is nearing the final stages. Some of his favorite influences include Edgar Allan Poe, Sylvia Plath, and Taylor Swift.

J.M. Recchia

Americano

Waiting for my Americano at Starbucks,
she entered the front door –
eyes locked to the floor.
Catching her from a side-glance,
with the cadence of a mourner leaving a gravesite,
by degrees she passed slowly behind me.
She wheeled a small double-basket shopping cart
with large white plastic bags stacked high –
like plowed pillows of snow after a whiteout.
Filled to the rim, on both top and bottom tiers,
the bags were placed thoughtfully and precisely in place –
as though they were pieces to a puzzle
that only she knew how to solve.
A few days from Halloween, she was dressed for winter.
A worn and frayed oversized wooly beige coat
drooped over her loosely, as it would a hanger.
She veered her seized belongings
to a vacant table towards the back,
sitting in a chair along side her creel of possessions.
The fingers of her hand –
like branches in winter –
thin and spindly –
gripped her pushcart with white-capped knuckles –
keeping a scrupulous and vigilant hold on it.
Making brief eye contact,
with a pensive smile –
gesturing for my attention,

her knobby index finger pointed towards me –
signaling me out of the handful of customers in the store.
I reticently made my way to her...
and was initially struck
by her unsullied beauty.
She was possibly in her mid-sixties,
her skin rose-pink, flawless as glass.
Her features diminutive and regal.
But behind her sapphire eyes
and sunless squinting gaze,
dwelled a penetrating emptiness.
"Would you be so kind as to buy me
a coffee please?" she asked in soft tones.
I responded to how'd she prefer it?
"A little cream, is all."
I ordered her coffee
handing it to her,
her sullen smile meeting mine –
she weakly uttered the words,
"God bless you."
I smiled in retreat
and headed to my car.
Sitting in the drivers seat –
I found my Americano Grande this day...
less than grand.

J.M. Recchia is a striving, not to be confused with starving writer. Although the latter would no doubt be the case, if not for the present means by which he procures the necessary provisions for his continued existence. He's a creative director for his own ad agency in Baltimore, MD. He's had numerous short stories and poems published by the Maryland Writers Association, the Maryland Bard Association and The Washington Writers Publishing House.

Kathryn Reilly

15th Century Rebellion

Masquerades
conquered the social construct
of monogamy
arranged for money, title, power, politics,
for brief interludes.

Keeping masks on
consenting adults swore
they didn't know their error(s).

But their hands knew the valleys
of their recorded vows
and relished exploring
new territory
living
for lavishly disguised
stolen moments
cleverly engineering
freedom of
choice.

By day, Kathryn helps students investigate words' power; by night, she resurrects goddesses and ghosts, spinning new speculative tales. Sometimes, she even writes the truth. Enjoy poetry in *Shadow Atlas, A Flight of Dragons, Last Girls Club, Willow Tree Swing* and fiction in *Tree and Stone, Seaside Gothic, Diet Milk, Blink Ink,* and *Fish Gather to Listen.* Her rescue mutts, Savvie and Roxy Razzamatazz, hear all the stories first. Twitter @Katecanwrite or katecanwrite.com

Carolyn L. Robinson

A Revolutionary Poem

I don't write poems about revolution
I have always been a love poet
Fancied kisses at sunset and long walks on beaches
Far more than I cared about democracy and talk about
The government

I cared more about making hearts smile than making friends
Across the aisle
I have always liked holding hands more than
Holding militant fists in the air
And every time the world demanded justice around me
I was always looking for love.
Always wondering how these two extremes could exist peacefully
In the same space.

While inequality painted clear pictures
Laid black and brown bodies out in the street
I looked for green spaces to bring us all together
I tried to make life imitate art
Because I don't know nothing about revolution
But I know at least twelve words that rhyme with care
So I keep pressing my agenda.

Keep telling you how to open your heart
How to use your words and not your fist
Figure out how to plant a garden in a bed of hostile soil
And still manage to grow beautiful yellow roses

And peace lilies
Cause all it takes is one seed
Planted, nurtured and cared for
to make all the difference in the world.

So I don't write poems about revolution
Can't pen what war is really like
But I know how hearts feel when two lovers collide
I know intimately how conflict between families puts up partitions
Like pins placed on a map of the world
Each one staking claim in their own territories
Fighting to create their own empires

I know how hate, unchecked, can build a war camp
Put up tent cities between people
just because of the color of their skin
with walls high enough that it would take a bomb to tear it down
Wouldn't that require a revolution?

Ain't that a war so cold when a gun placed between
any two irate ferocious hands
Can do the same thing
Set the same tone as opposing soldiers on a battlefield?
Ain't that an injustice?

When a body made in gods image grows a fury so strong inside
that love can't even live there anymore
Ain't that a gross miscarriage of some divine law too?

I told you I don't write poems about revolution
But if I did –
I would make sure they challenged you.
I would make you look for the god inside of you

And most of all,
I would make sure that they still end with love.

Terri Simon

Leftovers

A man who sleeps behind
the office building billboard
works the commuters in the morning.
He tells me he hunts jobs in the afternoon,
swears he'll be off
the streets by next winter.

Parents who carried their children
on their backs, walked away
from the rubble that had been home.
Traveling thousands of miles,
praying for an open door.

Children who sleep in an alley,
disowned by their righteous parents,
pay a price for being gay.
Refugees in their own land.

I want a table large enough
to feed them all.

Terri Simon's chapbooks are "Ringing the Bell," (Clare Songbirds Publishing House, 2021) and "Ghosts of My Own Choosing," (Flutter Press, 2017). Her work appears in "The Avenue," "Third Wednesday," "Poetry Quarterly," "Slant," and other print and online journals. She lives in Maryland. Find her at http://www.terricsimon.com.

Ginda Simpson

Tea upon the Terrace

The view paints itself
before my very eyes
Infused with light
Colors as soft
and transparent as
a watercolor
The blue of the sky
meets the sandy hues
of desert dunes
blushing rose
in the afternoon sun.

At river's edge
a graceful garden.
Tall palms pierce the sky.
slicing through the light,
their fronds leave
chiaroscuro shavings
across a lush lawn,
oleander and bougainvillea.
On the river
the white sails
of a felucca
catch the wind
propelling it

along the waters of the Nile
Transporting my thoughts
to Egypt's ancient past.

Tea upon the terrace
of the Old Cataract Hotel
is more than the ruby red
of hibiscus tea
sparkling gem-like in my glass.
More than the enamel
teapot that holds
the sweet scent of
fresh mint tea.

Tea upon the terrace
of the Old Cataract Hotel
is an infusion
of past and present.
A gift from the gods
offering me
in the stillness
of this present moment
the very essence
of this ancient land.

Enchantment.

Ginda is an artist, writer and dreamer of dreams. She has been a free-lance travel writer for a British journal produced in Egypt for ten years, and has published three illustrated personal memoirs, several collections of illustrated Italian travel memoirs and a cookbook. In her words, she pours out the contents of her heart in paintings, prose and poetry.

Dave Stant

A Song That Lives on Forever

There is a distance
between myself and others,
each thought an instrument
playing a song that
speaks to my innermost
fears hopes desires

Melodies can change
and from the moods they
create emerge themes
that tell a true story

The story is never complete
but if left unattended
its inspiration does not die
but grows stronger

A life, from wisdom gained,
touches lives and thus
echoes infinitely even
if unheard to the ear
of those who follow

My song will live on forever

Dave Stant is a poet from Maryland. His work has been featured in the 2020 and 2022 editions of Maryland Bards Poetry Review and was selected for inclusion in Train River Poetry Anthology Summer 2021. Dave has published one collection of poetry titled *Four Corners of Depression* (J2B Publishing, 2021).

Bernardo Taylor

Greening

Seeding
Feeding Land
In Hope That Beauty
Will Expand
Buds Of Peace
On Shrubs of Love
Open To Release This Fragrance
Around, Nearby, Above
In Traveling Winds Ascending
As Far As Faith Allows
Greening Of The Earth
We Now Know How

Brenardo, aka the Sing Song Poet is a resident of Prince Georges County. He currently holds the title as one of the Poets Of Excellence there. He has been writing poetry for over two thirds of his 60 plus year old life.

NORTH CAROLINA

Mary Bennett

Grateful

I've so much to be grateful for
But most of the time I don't try
I'm to absorbed in my own little world
To even stop and think why

I need to appreciate the little things
To look at my life and say
These moments make me happy
And be thankful each day

Originally from Birmingham in the UK, Mary Bennett moved to Durham, NC, 23 years ago and never looked back. Mary is currently battling Breast Cancer and poetry helps to deal with the hard days and gives her inspiration. Mary is an American citizen, wife, mother of 2 and has a very active Australian Labradoodle fur baby. Mary has been published in the North Carolina Bards 2021 and 2022 poetry anthologies. Mary loves hiking, photography and poetry and is looking forward to publishing more poems.

Christine Salkin Davis

Caught in Time

Squirming in darkness, a small
aromatic monstera,
far more than a leaf, a nodding,
a glistening,
like breath far away,
or a hastening, fallen stone,
biting wind, august air
beneath cumulus laying clouds.

Sky over lake glass,
masked muffed night sound,
her giggling voice,
talks on and on,
fearing not the rich,
caught between a cry,
fearing only men,
and boring angels fallen.

Christine Salkin Davis is an academic, poet, and artist from Concord, North Carolina. She is a Professor in the Communication Studies Department at UNC Charlotte, studying end of life communication in family, cultural, and political contexts. She writes poetry about her experiences with death and dying, spirituality, and social justice and compassionate living.

Lisa June Eames

The Fisherman's Dream

When he rises
feet spread wide
the hull
a trusty steed below
quavers and recoils

one glance
across the rippling water
a twist
back toward his net
one grab and spin
unfurling
begins

they fly
together
a spiral tangle
across the silver plane

and for a moment
suspended
above the depth
the shadow of the man
and net
forms a web across the waves

which moments later

joins itself,
a rhapsody
of man and sea

then through the scrim
but lovingly
the surface blinks
un-berthing him

Lisa June Eames is a poet, artist, and architect living on a mountain farm in Marshall NC. Poetry seems to stitch together the often divergent branches of past and present, of the mundane and the sublime; and acts as an interpreter of and connection to the world around us and within us.

Glenn Maughan

Whitebread Stew

Just like your mother never told you
more about the father you thought you knew
white bread stew is all about us
and all the neighbors and all the fuss

let's live without the labels
much too cumbersome for some i think
without your tag
its the not knowing
that makes you bad

white bread stew is easy
on the eyes and ears
but the mind is so hard to be pleased
cant get to it no matter what the fears

you keep it your way, the same way
everyone tries to be real
only thing that happens
is the same thing all over again

white bread stew is mixing
and the fixings about to start
come grip your plate of nothing
because the pot got gone no doubt

the trip is more about the trick
fool the many not just a few
cause some are alla bout plenty
we will miss our white bread stew

Glenn Maughan graduated from East Carolina University. He is a teacher at Central Carolina Community College and lives in Angier.

Nathan Nicolau

Death Follows Everyone, Not Me

No matter how many times
I could carve that into my throat,
I can't bring myself to say it.
Belief in Death is what drives us,
it's what keeps us kissing our children
or staying in our pasts.
It's your choice because despite what
all the poets and armchair philosophers
and tyrants say, Death does stop.
He stops at the loved ones,
the bystanders who never bothered,
the enemies who chant your name.
Death plays a rigged short game.
Suffering is the soul's cancer.

Nathan Nicolau is a writer/poet based in Charlotte, NC. His fiction, poetry, and essays have been featured in numerous websites and magazines. He is the founder and editor of New Note Poetry, an online poetry magazine.

Murali Sappa

Past

Fusing with the shadows of the past,
surfeit of hopes not lost,
musings linger, nudging one ahead –
and goals, a gleam in the eye, chased.

Past dawns with an intent to race
and frame the golden memories,
for walls of the future to grace.

Past, draws on an everlasting bounty
of experiences, serves you -
on the foggy dark path of fate,
staying with you to stay the course,
turning the journey of life
into a cruise through the milky way.

Forever, a shadow of the time, Past beckons
raising and nurturing today's hopes.

Past is nothing but a beacon,
a guiding Polaris of your future skies.

Murali Sappa is a seasoned computer professional whose interests include poetry and painting. The beautiful beaches and mountains of North Carolina, and the quirkiness of life fuels his imagination.

Joyce Thornburg

at the end of days

We bury our parakeet under
the tree outside our bedroom window.

As Granny consoles me, I swear
I see a halo around her head—

"I love you to the moon and back" she
whispers in my ear.

We sneak homemade moon pies into
our room under Mama's critical eye.

Granny calls me *Moon Beam* but it is she
who fills with light every night

as she reads to me from Revelations
until I can *see* the moon turn to blood.

SOUTH CAROLINA

Danny P. Barbare

Picking Blackberries

I'm going to pick blackberries, you can
come too.
They grow
in a red mud ditch
where bumblebees buzz on Queen
Anne's Lace and Ragweed in
bloom. The berries
are plump and juicy, stain
our fingers we lick, and the
bottom of the brown paper
bag. We'll take them home so my
wife can fix pie. It fills
the house with that heavenly aroma.
As it cools on the kitchen counter,
I can't wait for it to
melt in my mouth.
I'll have
to have a
another slice before
I'm satisfied. I'm sure you'll love it too.—

Danny P. Barbare resides in the Upstate of the Carolinas. His poetry has appeared locally and abroad. He attended Greenville Technical College and works at the University Center. He lives with his wife, mom, and misses his sweet dog Miley. His poetry has lately appeared in Pennsylvania Literary Journal and El Portal and New Feathers Anthology. He lives in Greenville, South Carolina.

Marie Griffin

Genesis

You are the only witness.

You are patient in the center
of your unseen universe--
a space between God's eyes.
Head down, black and yellow
legs unite in pairs.
Selective reflecting ultraviolet
light threads come together and
apart and back to the starting point.

The beginning is told
in a quantum zigzag band of silk.

You destroy and rebuild
silk masterpiece every night.
Majestic voyeur, cradle a century back
to a waking moment: another garden love story:
forbidden fruit, fight, and fallout.
Another woman marries mystery.

Vibrations set in another season.
The fabric begins and ends so
a moment will not forget what it had.

Your children emerge every spring
The wind scatters them.

They cannot see you.
They do not see themselves.
They drift through pockets of dust.

Peggy Shrum

A Walk Before Winter

She studies her steps
in the fallen leaves,
blinks away constellations
lost in galaxies,
and birds lost
in the light of the sun.
Every footfall airs
the trace of decay
the crisp and brittle sound
of another summer
dead beneath her feet.
Tender bent, tiny green,
beneath the littered leaves,
new shoots take shape
like question marks,
heavy-headed, waiting
to someday ask the sun
to raise them.

Peggy Shrum is a Wildlife Biologist living in the foothills of north-western South Carolina. Ms. Shrum is a bird watcher, an explorer, and a wilderness enthusiast. Her reverence for the natural world inspires her as an amateur poet and creative essayist.

KANSAS

Johnny Coomansingh

Mataburro

Back in the time
When I was hungry
In primary school
With one precious cent
Choosing to buy
A dab of peanut butter
On a piece of brown paper
Or a fat yellow
Mataburro banana
To fill the belly
Of a little fellow
A *donkey killer fig*
Ripped from a bunch
From the shopkeeper's counter
In my hand
It was grand
A "blessed" fruit to relish
Something for me to cherish
During the recess
With no shame I walked about
In the schoolyard
In those days
Things were difficult; hard
And my mother, so sad
In her penniless trouble
She knew of my struggle
But in glee I ate the *fig*

A fig normally thrown to fowl and pig
For my stomach called out
For something to reach my mouth
Because the single hops bread
Or piece of coconut bake and butter
To satisfy my hunger
Disappeared like raindrops on hot asphalt
This was the solution, a fat banana
Swallowed before the bell
Returning to my little *hell*
In a ram crammed seat
To face the *stench*, the heat
Thinking 'bout the mataburro
The *"killer of the ass"*
With a fear of the class
Until the next banana
Mañana, mañana…

Born in Sangre Grande, Trinidad and Tobago, Johnny Coomansingh started his work-life as a high school teacher. At this level he taught mathematics, human and social biology, regional geography and English composition. After eight years of teaching, he went to work as an agricultural extension officer spending nine years with the Ministry of Agriculture. In the United States he worked as a professor in the field of geography and tourism. Apart from the publication of several book chapters on tourism, he has authored the following books: *Sweet and Sour Trinidad and Tobago*, *Show Me Equality*, *Seven Years on Adventist Street*, *Cocoa Woman*, *An Understanding of the Trinidad Carnival*, and *Fifteen Christmas Poems and Some...* He is now the President of *"My Trinidad Yesterday, Today and Tomorrow,"* the only free online literary magazine in the Caribbean region (available: mytrinidad.net).

Anna Davies

Gas Lit

In the desert of purple sand
the running whales grew feet
that they slid into strappy sandals.
And on the seventeenth of June
In war-torn suburbia
the snow would not stop falling.
The accountants performed poetry
while lemurs in black berets
calculated the best ways to dance.
The people sank their toes into the clouds
and flowers showered down through
the crystal branches of sinking trees.
Gravity pulled the dolphins up from their beds,
and, thirsty, they drank the smoke
from shattered paper plates.
Sugar tasted too salty to swallow, so
Tongues craved the seasoning of milky gravel.
On this day, my mind was clear, so I
cleared my throat and spoke in charms
to everyone who listened.
To Everyone, who listened.
To everyone. Who listened?

Anna Davies is a teacher who lives in Lawrence, Ks with her loving fiancé
and five wildly creative kids. She has a Master's in English from Emporia
State University and has a passion for writing poetry and short stories.

Duanne L. Hermann

Waiting For Return

Rectangle of cement,
some foundation line,
homeless,
but love is evident:
bushes, flowers gone wild,
imported trees
and pump for water
under broken windmill,
plus a shed, leaning,
ready to collapse
as the family has
long, long ago.
Where are they now?
Married away?
Some, surely dead
in the cemetery near;
hope and money
exhausted.

A reluctant carbon-based life-form, Herrmann was surprised to find himself on a farm in Kansas and is still trying to make sense of that, but has grown fond of grass waving under wind, trees and the enchantment of moonlight. He aspires to be a hermit, but would miss his children, grandchildren and a few friends. His work has been published in print and online, even some of both in languages he can't read (English is difficult enough!). These include a sci fi novel, eight collections of poetry, a local history, stories for children, a book on fasting, plus other works. All this, and degrees in education and history, despite a traumatic, abusive childhood embellished with dyslexia, ADHD (both unknown at the time), cyclothymia, an anxiety disorder and, now, PTSD.

J.T. Knoll

raptured

out for
a morning
walk

i pass
at the
curb

slightly askew
some woman's
flipflops

that are
missing their
feet

wonder if
she got
raptured

by surprise
in her
housecoat

fresh cup
of coffee
steaming

as she
skipped over
death

rising up
to the
lord

surprised look
on her
face

as she's
not a
believer

TEXAS

Anne McCrady

The Hungry Season

In Sichuan's crowded cities,
cranes scrape and scavenge.
More concrete crumbles.
No one can stay inside.
Across China, car horns
herald the beginning of three minutes
of silence to mark the morning,
the hour, that shifting substrates
shoved rows of gray buildings to rubble
and grieving people to their knees.

An ocean away, a baby boy
wails from the arms of his sister,
as beside the road in Ghana,
they wait patiently as their prayers,
for a woman whose breasts
might still a blessing; their mother,
rendered dry by hunger
and well water too raw to swallow
because crops win the war for water.

In Myanmar, another week has passed
since a cyclone raked the valleys
and terraced hills. In villages
below, there is a rising flood
of fear talk as death joins destruction.
Bloated bodies raft the river.

Armed militia admit a trickle of aid.
The animals of abandonment roam
mud-laden paths as stunned people
gather, scavenge, go on living.

And in a crowded refugee camp, forgotten
fathers stare into their empty hands,
their bones brittle with exhaustion,
their feet, tired soldiers of exile,
their stomachs useless as clouds
that won't rain, in this, the worst
of the world's hungry season.

Anne McCrady is an award-winning poet and speaker, with decades of work published and presented in many genres. She is also a life-long social justice and peace advocate. She lives in Tyler, Texas.

MASSACHUSETTS

Holly Guran

Old Growth

How there is stillness, quiet
not a motor, not a boat on the lake.

Even the waves
merely lick the sand.

How the afternoon eagle arcs high
seeking the top of the pine.

The pine has been here since
Abenaki fishermen thrived,

their paddles stroking water
faintly heard,

the shoreline an encircling
of spruce, beech, fir,

a breeze so faint
the hemlock branches barely moved.

How the sleek loons glide
curving and dipping their black heads.

When gathered, they share
silent news of all they have been.

How there is stillness, quiet
not a motor, not a boat on the lake.

Holly Guran, author of *Twilight Chorus*, *River of Bones* and two chapbooks, earned a Massachusetts Cultural Council award and coordinates a popular Boston reading series. Her work has appeared in journals including *Poet Lore*, *Santa Fe Literary Review*, *Worcester Review*, and *Salamander*. *Harriet and Willliam*, based on the correspondence between a mill worker and the editor she married, is seeking a publisher.

Joshua Michael Stewart

Broken

A bird crashes against a window.
The children scream, the mother screams.

The bird's in the dirt flapping its broken wing
as the children run through the rooms

flapping their arms like wings, slam
into walls, smash into each other, whoop

and holler and laugh, and unsheathe their little teeth—
so tiny it seems they wouldn't break skin.

This house that smells like a woodpile
under a tarp after three winters,

where a social worker wrote in her notebook,
This mother clearly doesn't love this child,

where a river runs through the living-room,
and wildfires bloom in the bedrooms,

where there's something about my heart that isn't right,
and I'm an old rug left out over a porch railing in the rain,

where tomorrow will come, and I'll still be here
in one form or another, here where I can take off my shirt,

and bare the scar on my shoulder
that fits my younger cousin's mouth.

Joshua Michael Stewart is the author of Break Every String and The Bastard
Children of Dharma Bums. His poems have appeared in the Massachusetts
Review, Salamander, Plainsongs, Brilliant Corners, and many other publica-
tions. His third poetry collection, Love Something, will be published by Main
Street Rag. He lives in Ware, Massachusetts.

www.joshuamichaelstewart.com

OHIO

Brenda Arledge

No One Needs to Feel Hunger

Loneliness surrounds me,
no where do I see a smile
that's truly a friend,
as an emptiness feels the pit of my stomach.

I'm too proud to stand in line
waiting for a handout
when things will turn around,
after all, tomorrow the sun will surely shine.

No need to worry,
others are worse than me
with a family of four to feed,
I only wish I could lend a helping hand.

God willing,
I'll be back in the morning
with enough to take their hunger away,
at least, for one more day.

If not, I vow to be there
to stand for those in need,
because I know the feeling of hunger
is something no one needs.

Brenda Arledge is a poet residing in Ohio, of United States. She believes poetry is a turmoil of emotion comforting one's soul. Her poetry is published in numerous publications. She contributes regularly to Dimple Times, Hubpages.com & The Writers Club - Grey Thoughts.

Chuck Behrens

Never Endings

What I learned most
is that I didn't learn much
What I learned
I most likely forgot
sometimes instantly
or at least forgot to
Remember
It wasn't so much
Where are my Keys
Where'd I put my phone
Where's the remote control for the tv
The big lessons learned
"Don't worry, it will be ok"
"Be Kind"
"Don't take things so personally"
"Love is all"
"What matters, Matters"
"One out of One of us dies"
These are the Lessons
I had to take remedial classes
over and again
having past the Tests
written the Master Thesis
finishing the Doctoral Dissertation
how have I failed
to act as if I've never known
anything

to have to learn each of these lessons
once more
with the surprise of the pop quiz
given just for showing up
Damn It
What I have learned most
I didn't Learn much
I won't be commanded to repeat
to be held back
The Baccalaureate Ceremony
has already begun
Commencement can't be altered or stopped
Graduated
To What
To Where
To a Newness
Known
just not fully re-membered

Chuck Behrens is self-published author of Re-Member—A Memory Book, The Candle Maker and a recently published several chapbooks; he is national known speaker and a member of The National Speakers Association who works as a hospice chaplain and part-time minister. He resides in Bay Village, Ohio with his wife, Erin and deeply loves his five children and six grandchildren.

Linda Boerstler

Sunshine Springtime

Sunshine, springtime, sky
Blue like a blue-eyed girl
Smell of earth and life.

Cold finally breaks
Winter in a final bow
Time for new greening.

The first mow of grass
Sends perfume into the air
Sweet—like the first time.

Breathing fresh – fragrant
Scents of new bloom and rich soil
Windows wide-open.

Feeling young again
Just for a little while.
Healing my old soul.

Linda Boerstler has been a poet for as long as she has been able to write. There has always been a compulsion to record bits and pieces of her life into poems, or sometimes even stories, in an attempt to permanently capture the moment before it transforms itself into a memory. She has been published in several anthologies and just recently has self-published her first book Peregenius which is available as an Ebook on Amazon. More is yet to come. Linda has received an AA in Biblical Theololgy, a BA in Business Administration, a MPS in Christian Ministry and leadership and has been involved in some type of ministry over the years. She currently lives in Columbus, Ohio, her home town and shares her home with a very opinionated Jack Russell Terrier, Buddy, and an equally verbal Terrier mix, Kai. Both are from rescues.

Maureen Doallas

What Hungers Waits in Silence, Bidding

Gather dreams
and set them fast—

as lovers do
when dreaming's ended—

in resin thick,
no yellowed film

to cloud the past
made ever sweet.

We too did pry
from darkness once

what reasons not
in day's too cautious light.

What hungers
waits in silence, bidding

shadow from its lair.
What fears trails

remnants of a night
in search of lover's cache

encased. What murmurs
through the season done

is locust chiding touch
by light of moon,

her face as pinked
and delicate as bloom,

the cherry held
before her mouth

to tease a word
in one or other tongue.

To face un-shown
before a stone heart's

taunt, no palm
against a palm must trace

a ridge of brokenness,
nor steal from place too

tender yet the scent of silk
pulled up like dawn.

Fingers count by rosary beads
each body's treasure taken

till given thought no more.

Maureen Doallas's poems have been published in *The Strategic Poet* (Terrapin Books, 2021), *A Constellation of Kisses* (Terrapin Books, 2019), *The Dreamers Anthology* (Beautiful Cadaver Project, 2019), *Alice in Wonderland Anthology* (2015), and NOVA Bards' and other publications. Her debut poetry collection is *Neruda's Memoirs* (T.S. Poetry Press, 2011). Currently, she creates art exhibitions for her Virginia parish.

OKLAHOMA

LaVern Spencer McCarthy

Garden Sale

I sold a dozen villanelles today.
Each one was beautiful, unique and whole.
My sonnets went for more than most could pay.
I grew them in the garden of my soul.

Each one was beautiful, unique and whole.
My wild haikus were taken, row by row.
I grew them in the garden of my soul,
a special place that only I would know.

My wild haikus were taken, row by row
I planted them anew for later on.
A special place that only I would know
will care for them until their words have grown.

I planted them anew for later on.
The sunlight will caress them for awhile--
will care for them until their words have grown.
My poetry abounds with grace and style.

The sunlight will caress them for awhile.
I wrote them with the colors of the sky.
My poetry abounds with grace and style
with bright quatrains for sale to all who buy.

I wrote them with the colors of the sky.
My efforts made them somehow more divine.
With bright quatrains for sale to all who buy,
I polished them with joy and made them shine.

I wrote them with the colors of the sky.
My sonnets went for more than most could pay.
With bright quatrains for sale to all who buy,
I sold a dozen villanelles today.

LaVern Spencer McCarthy has been published in From the Shadows, a short story anthology edited by Amanda Steele, Uproar, and many others. Her poems have appeared in numerous state and national anthologies. She resides in Blair Oklahoma.

UTAH

Carolanna Lisonbee

Ghost Sustenance

I trace the branching lines of my palm
not sure if I'm looking for a lifeline or a ghost.
When the line of your life becomes fluid,
the bitterest things, so long as they're solid, are sustenance.
A liquid life settles in whatever space
it's given, even if it's just between the pages of a book.

How would I put it if I were writing this book?
What turns of phrases would I palm?
I broadcast my feelings into outer space,
where they might be caught by a passing ghost.
For the dead, I imagine, living moments are sustenance.
Even boredom, even misery is a vital fluid.

Every day you work to exhaustion and collapse like your body's a fluid.
If you catalogued your grievances they would fill a book.
You're starving because no one taught you what a soul needs for sustenance.
Resting your face in your hands, something wet touches your palm.
You never got that old saying, "give up the ghost,"
yet here you are, reminding yourself you're nothing but haunted dust floating
in space.

Beyond the bright blue sky are hidden the diamond stars of space,
and the ocean looks like platinum turned to fluid.
The memory of normal life is nothing but a ghost.
You are here, on a beach, holding a good book,
in the shade of a breeze-possessed palm.

It reminds you you're a living thing, with sunlight for sustenance.

Where can I turn for sustenance?
When all I ask is a little space,
I'm answered with a slap from an open palm.
Blood and tears—if only my assets were equally fluid...
Oh, the flights and hotel rooms I'd book.
He'd look for me, but I'd be a ghost.

Like everyone else, you'll end up a ghost,
free of all that life demands you sacrifice for sustenance,
remembered, if at all, like a footnote in a book,
but what's yours in return is the vastness of space.
Your atoms will scatter in a dance, you'll become fluid,
stardust caught in some future far distant child's palm.

envoi

Your soul is a ghost: give her some space.
Treasure your daily sustenance, both solid and fluid.
Write your joys in a book and your sorrows on your palm.

Carolanna Lisonbee is a writer, English teacher, and globetrotting adventuress from Utah. Her poems and translations can be found in TEA-KU: POEMS ABOUT TEA, by Local Gems Press, and The Whiskey Blot, and the journal Reliquiae, issue 10.1, published by Corbel Stone Press. She posts on Instagram as carolanna_joy_poetry, and writes #ScienceNewsHaikus on Twitter as @carolannajl.

CALIFORNIA

Ava Bird

Home of the brave

shine your light
don't dim it
don't give into pressures
of others little thoughts, judgments, criticism
petty beasts
don't fall for it
shine your best
and light the way forward
onward
 flip them the bird metaphorically
and keep running ahead and learning
 stay ahead of the game
away from those mind numbed masses
those masses of asses
vaccinated minds tv sets demented thoughts
fake foods burger murders slaughterhouses
profits plus prophets
pocketing
leaves us sick and desperate
fear and porn
they can be so obscene
but we can do better
we as humans
together as a race
I promise
We can build communities
nice homes

community gardens and clean water for everyone
no question
homes for the brave
for the sick and disabled
 we should all live freely and happily
safely and freely for all beings
 yes, all of us happy and free
home of the brave
and the courageous gorgeous souls
living and passing
passing the torch
the torches of light and fire
the brave and the shining
enlighten the way forward

Ava Bird is a multi-dimensional artist whose work appears in academic journals, historical anthologies, in art galleries, online and in international publications. She lives in gratitude on and for Mother Earth.

Drew Campbell

Shadow Sentry

The little sentience,
In the unsettling shadow,
Hears the jingles,
And falls to order.

Called from,
And to,
Every edge,
And boundary.

A loyal shred of darkness,
Guided by familiar noises.
Reaching the post,
To receive troves of gratitude.

Repetition,
Predictable,
And tame.
A silent sense of security.

Drew Campbell is a writer & artist from California. Together with his partner, he runs **VLASINDA PRODUCTIONS.** Their focus is on creating artwork in multiple mediums, as well as organizing events and platforms to help other creatives network and showcase their work.For more information and updates, visit **IG: @vlasinda_stormdrain** & **YouTube.com/vlaSINda**

Timothy Paul Evans

An Archive in the Attic

considers ephemera
and connotations coaxed
out of hiding, the ripped
knees of jeans exposing the
long forgotten, coming to
asymmetrical terms with the
uncomfortable positions taken
by the hardcore moments of the
day; Eisenhower jackets, bell
bottom pants and a three ring
circus of headlines from
Manson to Saigon, lives dressed
up, lives gone down, the heaving
of breasts breathing in the mustiness
of departures not so well rehearsed

Timothy Paul Evans began writing poetry about fifteen years ago. His poems have appeared in several anthologies including California Quarterly, the 2020 San Diego edition of Bards Against Hunger, Trees in a Garden of Ashes and CHAOS, BEAT-itude National Beat Poetry Festival 10 Year Anthology, We Are Beat, National Beat Poetry Foundation Anthology. Also in the 2018-2019 Summation 2020-2021and the 2021- 2022 San Diego Poetry Anthology. He also has two new chapbooks; "Gertrude Stein's Rose" and "Something in the Water". His full length book of poetry, "Litanies of the Moon", will arrive later this year.

Joseph Milosch

Bells of Mercy

Saint Mary's bells call the hour.
The sky darkens over Dublin,
and I walk in Purnell Square,
looking at the narrow streets
and thin buildings. Black, clouds
foretell rain, and the crowd
parts for the shoeless woman.

Crying, she comes down the street,
wearing a checkered shirt,
threadbare jeans, and a pair
of pink socks. Her blond hair
has streaks of gray and
is unkept as if she slept
behind the hedgerows.

She walks in front of me, turns,
stepping into the wall of a pub.
She bounces off and spins
before leaning against the stone
window frame. Placing her face
in the crook of her arm,
She resembles a runner
stretching her hamstrings.

"I just want a cup of tea.
A bloody cup of tea,"

she wails before sobbing
and talking to anybody,
but nobody listens.
When the rain begins,
the bells continue to ring
without mercy.

Leaning against the pub's wall,
her shoulders shake
as she cries while the bells
continue their cold,
metallic chime of coins,
calling people to teatime
in Dublin.

Joe Milosch's new book is *A Walk with Breast Cancer*. His book *Homeplate Was the Heart & Other Stories* was nominated for the American Book Award and the Eric Hoffer, best Small Press Publication. His other books are *The Lost Pilgrimage Poems & Landscape of a Woman and a Hummingbird*.

Peg Rose Pawlak

Cobwebs

I see a cobweb hanging from the lampshade.
It embraces the lamp light like an actor on stage
with the spotlight focused on every move made.

It is sticky to the touch,
and wraps around my fingers.
I pull at it, shake it away, wad it into a ball—

it still holds tight to my palm
like cotton candy at the fair
when you miss your mouth,
and it globs in your hair.

Above my head a cobweb clings,
up in the corners of the ceiling.
Gently it sways in puffs of air
that seem to be blowing in
from everywhere.
It hangs there
looking like a miniature harp string
ready to be plucked.

I must admit
I would like to catch
that eight legged loom
that left them here.

Peg hails from beautiful San Diego, California. She is a retired USAF Veteran and substitute teacher. Peg is married to Joseph, and has one cat named Hermione. She is proud to participate in this Bards Against Hunger ten year anthology.

Barbara Simmons

Escape Plans

We do it without thinking, sighting those red block letters,
                    EXIT
reassuring our leaving places we have found ourselves,
or, more precisely, where we've found ourselves lost,
in theaters, malls, relationships,
those gathering spaces where,
not sure sometimes why we're there,
we fold away small notes to self, including routes by which we'll leave.
It's been a year since we took leave
from what? Routines, connections, worn out paths of
customary comings, anticipated goings,
a year of changing patterns, forswearing the habitual,
creating novel ways to meet, to share, to love, to spend
time trying not to think where we should have been,
envisioning new plans to leave the here and now
without abandoning ourselves. What's left
when signs are not available? The word itself lies next to
others in the dictionary, including existential,
become new guides for taking leave, and flight, and hold
of who we are
as we discover what
it is to paint our own way out of boxes, out of corners,
over all walls that restrict our freedoms
finding what we've missed seeing, how we've missed living.

Barbara Simmons lives in California and relishes celebrating all that she associates with life - joy, sorrow, care, relationships - with her poetry. A graduate of Wellesley and Johns Hopkins' Writing Seminars, Barbara has been a teacher and counselor, a guide and mentor, a published poet. Most especially, she is a mother and grandmother, hoping that her words will continue to help not only her family, but the world, understand, more, life itself.

Mary Langer Thompson

Surreal Cup of Joe

I'm left in the café with a cuppa,
upset from a conversation
with my erst-while friend, when I
hear a voice from the next table.

He's alone, reading aloud
in a brilliant British accent:
You rather than thank me, ruin my heart.
He pauses, smiles slightly, hand on cheek.

Shakespeare? Dante? I can't see the cover.
His only audience remains himself
and me—although he's not aware
and doesn't seem to care who might be staring.

I don't want to ask him. I've approached
enough totally mad people in my life.
She wanted to reign 'til the end of her days.
Now we're getting to the nub of the matter.

Dangerous to approach. Doubly dangerous.
The engrossed man laughs, shakes his head.
Enough! He reads with expression.
Is he a frustrated actor, author? Is he sane?

I rise and walk past him, striving to see a title.
He's still reading, clutching the book.

Break off that crazy bond. He looks up at me:
Keep your head now.

I nod. *I'll try, Sir. I'll try.*

Mary Langer Thompson is a contributor to two poetry writing texts, *The Working Poet* (Autumn Press, 2009) and *Women and Poetry: Writing, Revising, Publishing and Teaching* (McFarland, 2012), was the 2012 Senior Poet Laureate of California, and was recently nominated for a Pushcart Prize.

Chris Vannoy

Harvest

He sat hooded
The long-handled scythe
Lying restlessly
Across his dark robed lap
Ivory teeth dangling
In a half smiling rosary about his neck

"It's been a good year!",
He said to himself
Jingling the treasure of bones
In his pocket
Coins of the dead, spent lives,
Fuel for the funeral fires
To keep him warm
Against the chill of winds
That moan with the cry
Of those still tied to the earth
They had waited long for him
To end the ceaseless
Procession of days upon days
Scratching handfuls of earth
Spooning out pieces
Of ground to lie in
As he sits,
And waits, and laughs, and rises
Swishing the curved blade
One, two, one, two

Reaping his crop while it is ripe
Then he laughs

And sits, and counts
One, two, one, two

He was the Beat Poet Laureate of California 2018 and the United States Beat Poet Laureate in 2019. During those years he completed 2 tours of Europe. Last year he was invited to attend the TANTA poetry Festival in Tanta, Egypt. This year he was given the Beat Poet Laureate Lifetime award

VERMONT

Jay Hall Carpenter

Gleaning

Her: scratching stubbled cornfields with the crows
To fill a needy pocket in the bleak.
A few dry kernels fallen in the rows—
A gnawing, woeful game of hide-and-seek.
Them: digging desert roots in brittle soil
With fly-vexed baby hanging in her sash,
Too dry to nurse the child or to toil,
And all too weak to pound the root to mash.
Him: crumpled in the frigid alley doorway
Waiting for the restaurant close,
Praying for enough for just one more day.
Asleep before the cup of coffee froze.
And none of these will see another dawn,
But Hunger will go gleaning, on and on.

Jay Hall Carpenter has been a professional artist for over 40 years, beginning as a sculptor for the Washington National Cathedral. His books include *Dark and Light, Poetry* (2012); *101 Limericks, Inappropriate For All Occasions* (2017); and *Model Home Poems* (2021). He now creates in Charlotte, VT.

FLORIDA

Joanne Alfano

Fear and Silence

Somewhere, cages of lonely, terrified children
cry for their parents and fear for their lives.

Somewhere, day and night,
children of war seek safety from bombs
that blast through homes, hospitals, schools

In broad daylight
between multiplication tables and vocabulary
school children endure active shooter drills
and far too often, active shooters

A pregnant woman's fetus is protected.
her child, especially if she is poor,
bears little political concern.

In plain sight
children drink lead-poisoned water
that eats their brains and stunts their growth.

At night
in the world's wealthiest countries
children go to bed hungry.

Under a starry sky
a man walks into a dark room, touches a child,
and rapes that child into silence.

Children have become prey --
trophies for politicians, hunters, predators,
and mass murderers.

Civilization left the children behind
in cages, dark rooms, bombed cities,
countries decimated by disease and famine.

Civilization has been left behind
Now fear lurks in plain sight, and
silence pierces the global night.

Joanne Alfano has two poetry collections: *Soul Tracks* (2020) and *dreams drumbeats heartbeats* (2022. Her work has appeared in periodicals and journals, including The Dew Drop, several NOVA Bards Anthologies, The Wisconsin Review, and The 10th Anniversary Bards Against Hunger Anthology. After a career as an information systems project manager, she retired to Florida to enjoy family, writing, reading, and watching classic movies.

Karen Koven

Inspiration

Eight weeks old, five pounds.
The first time, they put you in my arms
you were a ball of white fluff
curled in on yourself.
You must have been confused, "who are these people?"
Your only discernable parts were
a chunk of coal nose and black searching eyes.
Eyes that did not know me;
my heart knew you.

Twelve weeks, eight pounds.
When the amber morning light chases shadows across the room,
you sense us stirring.
Drowsy you nestle between our pillows.
My fingers reach for the baby-soft
tendrils of your curly hair.
Earthy and fresh,
I breath in the smell of you
like summer rain and dandelions,
like a love-worn teddy bear.
Squirming between the two of us you trumpet
your staccato bark, begging for our attention.
Simultaneously we rub your tummy.

Sixteen weeks, twelve pounds.
Morning yoga, why do I even try?
As soon as I stretch out on the floor

your immediate and exuberant pounce
has you standing over me, one paw on each shoulder.
Wild and scratchy, your retriever-sized tongue
burrows into my face and neck.
Wet nose to my nose.
You make me laugh. The house quivers with joy.
The world is bright.
Today I will write happy poems.

Karen Koven is an author living in Clearwater Fl. Her focus is Poetry and Micro Memoires. She was awarded first-place in the Romeo Lemay Poetry Competition, 2017. Her career as a Senior Consultant with an international training and development company spanned more than two decades. She has been published in journals and anthologies.

Vincent J. Matsko

Not Quite

Heironymous Sludge
And Phineas Phipp
    Did hop aboard
    Their sailing ship.

They went 'round the world
Not once, but twice --
    And almost went
    Around it thrice.

Alas, they encountered
The same problem as I,
    They ran out of steam.

Vincent J. Matsko lives on a remote bluish planet in the Milky Way Galaxy. After doing a bunch of stuff other people told him to do for a while, he's pretty much his own boss now. He writes puzzle books, teaches a calculus class, participates in a writing circle (where he's working on a stage play), and designs digital artwork. He loves fish pie.

Judith Rosner

Pick Up at P.S. 261

Like a well-orchestrated stage performance
set to the music of children's laughter,
each class takes its appointed space in the schoolyard.
Young students score a spot on the grass,
While children in older grades cluster around them.
Teachers stand sentry.

Outside a chain link fence wait parents,
grandparents, nannies, and younger siblings.
All look excitedly for their charges through
the diamond shaped spaces in the fence.
Some have their fingers laced through the wire
and add to the happy hubbub by waving or calling to their child.

At precisely 2:42 the fence gate swings open.
En masse, the chaperones flood the schoolyard,
and like water flows through a slot canyon,
they grasp their child's hand, exit
by a gate on the opposite side of the yard,
and spill onto the street to a chorus of goodbyes.

As I put my arms around my grandson,
My responsibility this day,
I can't help but think what would happen
if a person with a gun and vengeance on his mind
should show up at pick-up time.

Judith Rosner, Ph.D., writes poetry and creative non-fiction. Her work appears in the literary journal HerWords, the Living Peace 2019 Art of Poetry Anthology, the Jewish Writing Project, the Gulf Coast Poets/Florida Bards Poetry Anthology, and the Jewish Literary Journal. She began writing after a successful career as sociologist, leadership trainer, and executive coach. Judy and her husband split their time between Sarasota, Florida and New York City.

COLORADO

Zaneta Varnado Johns

Hunger, a Global Tragedy

Hunger happens when humanity fails
Our most basic human need—unmet
Swollen bellies, empty stomachs
Desperate souls—abandoned
Eyes wide open, no hope in sight
Clean hearts, dire circumstances
People are starving!

The tragic contrast is an abomination
Tunnel vision void of compassion
Deep pockets, too-full bellies
Greedy souls, willful waste
Blind society, access denied
Blissful hearts, luxuries abound
People are satiated!

It is not too late to help
the helpless
the hopeless
the homeless
the hungry

Malnutrition is a human condition
Silent cries—weak, shaky, and lightheaded
A global cacophony of growling stomachs—
Inhumane
Stop, look, and listen

People are dying!

It is almost too late
for far too many!

MISSOURI

Michael H. Brownstein

The Children Are Hungry

I woke alive this morning
flesh of cabbage piled on the kitchen counter
the dogs resting behind their barricade
outside, a Monsanto blue

the snare drum still needs a resting place
green leaves sparkling nearby
a dozen volunteers laughing and ready
fresh water bottles everywhere

some days the sun misses the point
Pine Ridge gathers itself in shadow and pollutants
we stack the boxes of food onto the cargo bed
the truck rusty and torn

and head to the grocer across the state line
pass out food to anyone who wants some
listen to the anger of the greedy store manager
and tell the people we will be back everyday

we live near and we live far away
welcome warriors joining our effort
ponder over a gallon of milk costing seven dollars
and how greed has more value than hunger

Michael H. Brownstein's latest volumes of poetry, *A Slipknot to Somewhere Else* (2018) and *How Do We Create Love* (2019) were both published by Cholla Needles Press.

WASHINGTON

Linda Conroy

A Little Mercy

There may be look-outs in high-rises,
people planning desperate deeds.
There may be famine, fire, fear, flood
and furloughed workers unable to afford to eat,
and sickness with high fever, lack of breath,
lying face down in a bed, or sleeping outside
in a tent, with rain and snow, no toilet, no toothbrush,
no way to find the only space left in the heat.

Dread, doubt and despair, scorn, derision
lay new-found discomfort, wrapping those
who don't need a new vision or a blinding light,
but a hard-boiled egg warm in their hand.
a mug of soup, a pair of socks, a towel
a blanket, your old creaky folding chair,
or catch their eye with more than words,
a crooked smile to bring their spirits near.

Linda Conroy likes to write about the complexity of the behaviors that make us human, and influence our connection with the natural world, especially in these times of change. Her work has appeared in many journals and she is the author of a poetry collection, *Ordinary Signs*.

ILLINOIS

Kari Hilmanowski

Finally

I'm on the right path,
the dirt beneath my feet
and the emerald green grasses
tickling my ankles.
I close my eyes
as the sun warms my skin
and I take a deep breath,
inhaling the earth
deep into my belly,
deep into the unknown parts
of who I am,
as I wonder where I'm headed.

Kari Hilmanowski has recently returned to the Midwest, settling in Illinois. She enjoys watching the local birds, rabbits, and cornfields, and spending time with her best buddy, a small Chihuahua named Bosley.

MICHIGAN

Sandra Place

The Injured Musician

The music drifted down the hallway,
Softly and gently,
His voice was soothing,
A gentle tune in a sorrowful time.
He sang alone, unaware of anyone hearing him.
He sang to whomever or whatever was listening,
But mostly it seemed, he sang for himself.
As he left the building, he limped,
His leg, plaster cast and awkward.
He struggled with the awkwardness,
He limped on and he smiled,
Still humming his tune.

Sandra Place lives a life rich in experience and education. She holds a master's degree in counseling psychology, a graduate certificate and various other certifications in holistic health. She is a healthcare consultant and educator and utilizes creative approaches to the provision of care. For more, find her at www.asandyplace.com.

NEBRASKA

Nathanael Urie

a gingerbread hang glider (for Charlie Chaplin)

if he was in Pamplona
during Running of the Bulls,

a Longhorn hooks a beltloop
and lifts him off the stoop

trampling at full speed,
he'd spread his arms like a hang glider

busying himself with knitting needles
as he dangled,

a few moments to macrame,
he'd unfurl a Spanish flag

or clip at folded cardboard to reveal
an outstretched chain of gingerbread men

Nathanael Urie lives in Lincoln, Nebraska. In April, Urie wrote his first poetry chapbook, *The Happy Year,* a slapstick about Charlie Chaplin. Five poems appear in *Glasgow Review of Books.*

MINNESOTA

Vincent O'Connor

Grief

she circles disconsolately
then stops

trunk waving up and down
ears half-forward
she cautiously approaches him
temporal glands streaming
in poignant mourning

she stops intermittently
allowing her trunk tips
to compassionately caress
his jaw
his tusks
his teeth

and tenderly places one foot
on his alabaster skull
to rock it back and forth

in time she tears grass clumps
and gathers dead branches
to reverently enshroud his carcass

keeps muted vigil for
a night and a day

then withdraws from
the consecrated ground
to walk in sorrow
towards the waiting heard

Vincent O'Connor's debut poetry chapbook, Lessons From Life, was published by Local Gems Press in 2019. His poems have appeared in Snail Mail Review, The Talking Stick, Main Channel Voices, Winamop, Poetry Super Highway, Satori, and elsewhere both in print and online. He lives in Minnesota, and works with computers for a living but writes for life.

TENNESSEE

Suitin Li

No more hunger or thirst

On that day
when the Son of Man
takes His bride home
He will wipe away
every tear from their eyes

In their new home
they'd say goodbye
to their worries and pain
there will be no more hunger or thirst
for the Son of Man
will give them a living water

Suitin Li is a graduate student at Lipscomb University, pursuing a Masters degree in Education. She is also currently a pre-school teacher and she loves to write in her free time. She loves poetry because it expresses one's emotion and their life journey.

<u>INTERNATIONAL</u>

UNITED KINGDOM

Cathy Bryant

I Want One

Some facet of brakes or wheels strikes sparks
from the cobbles and the boy whoops and laughs
as his mother bumps the wheelchair along.
"Like a fairground ride!" she beams at me
and I smile back, doing my crutches-waltz
over the uneven stones, each unique like faces
or fingerprints, with gentle moss between.

The sound and feel of crutch and feet:
clack-thud on the cobbles, silent softness
on moss, transmitted up to my arms.
The wheelchair sounds like a zipwire or train.

A girl, about six, is being dragged along by
her mother, her little legs reluctant. She looks
at the wheeling laughing boy in his sparking
chariot and tugs at her mother's hand: "Mam!
Look, Mam! See that? I want one! I want one!"

After being homeless in her teens, Cathy Bryant worked as a life model, shoe shop assistant, civil servant and childminder before writing professionally. She has had hundreds of poems and stories printed all over the world, and also won 33 literary awards. See Cathy's listings for impoverished writers at www.compsandcalls.com/wp

Julia Davenport

Soundscapes

What is music?
Its mystical power will transform
Like the pendulum voiced hypnotist.
Songs evoke Polaroid photos mind trapped.
Music to dance to
Egyptian Sand dance, Chinese Lion dance, Indian Bhangra,
And Indonesian Balinese. Music to sing to
Love songs that hug you
While Football chants fuel you.
Music to make love to
'Sexual Healing'
Will entice and seduce you.
Music to protest to
Dylan and Marley's rage against racism
Like Political movements moving mountains
With musical mindfulness.
Music to cry to
Rhythmic, harmonic, melodic Blues
Empathise when the world caves in on you.
Music to boost you
Like 'I will survive'
When a lover has left you.
Music to chill to
New Age sounds of birdsong and
Waves to still the mind to.
Music to marry and
Wedding March down the aisle to.

Music to be born to
'Happy Birthday'
To dance down the love canal to.
Music to be buried to
Gregorian chants
Move your soul to heaven
As the angels guide you.
Music to be downloaded to iPods
Like black magic boxes
Holding music makers captive in digitised prisons.
Hip hop DJs scratching and rapping in my ears so clear,
And B-Boys breakdance mind pictures of yester year.
Sound and music is all around,
The soundtrack to life.
So live, love and listen to the sound.

Julia Davenport is a freelance author and poet. Born in Salford in 1977, she now lives in Manchester in the northwest of England, UK. Julia holds a BA(Hons) English Language and Literature degree and is currently studying for an MA in Creative Writing with The Open University. Since 2010 her work has been widely published in many anthologies, exhibitions, and magazines. In 2017 her first poetry collection Order & Chaos: a collection of protest poems was published by Ragiel & Gill Press.

Candi M

Food Bank

At Half-Term now we buy
All Butter Flapjacks,
satisfying flip tops
syrupy delights.
We fill our boot with deep green bags
of delicacy,
we hit the road on holiday.
I watch electronic wing mirror
swish, my daughter savours godly snacks,
I silently count our blessings,
feel the ache it took to get here.

In 1989, I awoke one day to a
humming fridge filled with half a cabbage,
some moulding jam,
three torn slices of stale white bread.

An empty pressure cooker of corned
beef hash sat crusting on our old hob.
Hot cross buns with half-ripped
clearance stickers,
an attempt to hide the food bank.

We would
sneak much bigger
10 pence pieces from permed hair grown-ups,
hide them under Polly Pocket pillowcase,

peg it to the corner shop
a rainbow wall of perforated boxes,
Beef Potato Puffs for breakfast.
On the tummyache walk to school,
lollipop man Jim
placed one wrapped Opal Fruit into each of
our small
palms.
Strawberry was my favourite day.

Our food at home sent from supermarkets onto
charity just as it began to rot,
next onto our bellies.
In class our desperate toilet calls
always met with
wait til playtime.

Candi M is a tutor from the UK. She completed MA Creative Writing for Wellbeing during the Pandemic and and delivers local workshops. She loves music, nature and huge cups of tea. Publication with Fragmented Voices, South Bank Poetry, MONO Fiction and others. Instagram @candi_says_

Rob Walton

Bank

Write poems on the tins you put in the foodbank
Write verse about how foodbank even became a word
Write about alternatives to foodbanks
Write long lines about love conquering all
Write about love not necessarily being a short-term
solution for the starving
Write that then again maybe love is the answer
Write about protest and togetherness
Write advice about where to get better advice
Write the ingredients for a revolution on a packet
of something indulgent
Write about the need for treats
Write about the need for levity and seriousness
Write about us and them
Write about whether there is ultimately only us
Write about rights and responsibilities
Write about ending austerity and words of plenty
Write about writing a Closed sign on the last foodbank.

Rob Walton is from Scunthorpe, and now lives in Whitley Bay, England. His poems, flash fictions and short stories for adults and children have appeared in various anthologies and magazines in several countries. Arachne Press (UK) published his debut poetry collection, This Poem Here, in March 2021. He sometimes tweets @robwaltonwriter.

CANADA

Agnes Bellegris

Playing Pretend

The toys were packaged
With love by a mother
Who wasn't ready to
Say goodbye to the children
Who used to play with them.
It was a rainbow zoo of stuffies
And vehicles. They were the
Essence of naivety when aside from
A jealous swipe and hair pull of
"It's mine" meant memories of
Innocence when playing pretend
Was a serious activity.
Watching them was fun
Mostly. Sitting on the floor with them
Counting, reading, pointing, chatting
To a clockless day then
Singing the "clean up" song
Was a daily ritual
She never envisioned would end
As abruptly as it did.
Today the toys sit in storage.
She's held onto them for so long.
A new home through the donation bin
Isn't in their future. She wants to touch them
And sniff them and hold on to those fleeting years.
The elders told her she would miss it. She wasn't sure
she believed those words. She believes them now.

The toys are staying waiting for a child
To come and love them again.

Agnes Bellegris is from Ontario, Canada. She is an editor by trade who thinks in snippets. This makes her well-suited to writing poetry.

Glenda Walker-Hobbs

Lessons From Hunger

The stocky, overweight minister and his wife
travel to Haiti for missionary duty,
take lots of canned food supplies with them.
After meals, they hear a strange noise by the garbage,
find people fighting over empty cans.
The minister looks at his adipose belly.
Waves of guilt wash over him.
He and his wife hide in the closet for meals,
leave food in the cans for garbage scroungers.
Soon they live on one meal a day.
The minister loses weight rapidly.
By the end of the missionary stint,
he has lost sixty pounds.
He returns home deeply shaken by his experience.
He starts a food bank at his church.

Glenda Walker-Hobbs (Glennis Hobbs) is a Canadian poet and writer. She helped found a local Writers Guild and currently serves as its secretary. She is a long-time member of Writers Village University. She is a co-moderator of the Poetry Study group there as well as a member of the Julia Cameron Study Group. She is working on her MFA in Poetry there. She has published eleven books of poetry, including nine chapbooks. She has had prose and poetry published in various anthologies and e-zines including Village Square (villagesquareliterary.com). She currently has two poetry books and two novels in progress. She has a poetry web page at
https://gwalkerhobbs.angelfire.com/

Tanya Adèle Koehnke

Slinky

my silver Slinky
springs into action
somersaults downstairs
a flight of twelve steps

boing-boing-boing
boing-boing-boing
boing-boing-boing
boing-boing-boing

tumbles onto the floor
a spiral of wires
a toy acrobat
motionless

Tanya Adèle Koehnke earned her MA in English from York University. Tanya taught English at several colleges and universities in Toronto. Tanya also has a background in arts journalism. Tanya's poems appear in *The Ekphrastic Review*; *The Ekphrastic World Anthology 2020*; *Framed & Familiar: 101 Portraits*; *Hamilton Arts & Letters'* "The Canadian Chapbook" issue; *Canadian Woman Studies; Poets & Painters; The Canvas; Big Art Book; tinted memories* (Third Iris Zine); *Sleet Magazine; Foreplay: An Anthology of Word Sonnets; Tea-Ku: Poems About Tea; Grid Poems: A Guide and Workbook*; ***Alchemy and Miracles: Nature Woven Into Words***; and other publications.

Honey Novick

"It" Found Me
"it" found me
the voice – soft, rhythmic, morphing
a story, a narrative
"it" found me
"it" told me they saw me
"it" told me it was female
"it" told me they saw my rotten mood
"it" told me "it" was poetry and poetry was my friend

"How", I queried,
"You who are atmosphere, oxygen, gas?"

"it" posited, then replied = "we are all one
poetry lives in hope
poetry sees you can use some hope
you are in a rotten mood, sad, despairing"

It said, "remember,
being alone
even feeling alone
doesn't mean being lonely
think about that"

i thought and observed and pondered
sitting by the lake
noticing the swans no longer come to this shore
they have moved their nesting ground
a sign posted said this part of the shore

is now a place to spread funeral ashes
the swan's home has always been sacred
they found a new place to birth life
leaving the old for memories of ancestors

the rain will come
all will be cleansed and soaked
poetry will breathe new hope into the world

Honey Novick is a singer/songwriter/voice teacher/poet living in Toronto, Canada. Her writing has been translated into Spanish, Japanese, Urdu and French. She has been published in numerous anthologies and has ten chapbooks and eight CDs. She is the 2020 recipient of the Mentor Award (CSARN) Canadian Senior Artists Resource Network, 4-time awardee of the Dr. Reva Gerstein Legacy Fund, and recipient of the 2020 and 2022 Community Hero Award. She is a resource artist for the Friendly Spike Theatre Band and teaches Voice Yoga.

Charlotte Sachs

Memory Loss

Do not walk boldly,
Circle through it with a greedy reverence.
It is a meditation path with no end destination,
The overgrowth of childhood reaching out to scratch calves; tendrils of wild
blackberries,
Tender and tangy purple that tastes like Berkshire summer,
Tiptoe past the clear cuts of memory's absence –if I am quiet enough, I might
catch a fleeting look:

Cold red tile kitchen floor,
Mesh sides of a playpen pressed into the skin of ticklish palms,
Zodiac patterned cotton of a woman's robe,

The empty clearcuts carve jagged stripes into the dappled landscape..
It is hard to trust the well-intentioned woodman that cut them down,
Evicting wraiths and wolves by cutting down the trunks that cast shadows to
hide them.

Meditate on the Baby and the bathwater,
Dumped over wet pink sneakers that can never be sure what they are running
from.

Charlotte Sachs is a twenty-five year old poet who grew up in rural Massachusetts learning to love the rhythms and stories of the natural world around her. The last six years were spent making British Columbia up in Canada her home, and writing stories and poems that help her to make sense of an ever-changing world. She is now a MFA student at Naropa University's Jack Kerouac School of Disembodied Poetics.

AUSTRALIA

John Hansen

Just A Tramp

Sitting on a park bench
Watching life pass by,
Patches on his jacket,
Doesn't own a tie.

Tattered pants and worn-out shoes,
A bottle of the cheapest booze.
He doesn't have a social class,
A sign says "Please Keep Off The Grass."

Once he dined on home-cooked meals,
Roast chicken, apple pie,
Now he raids the litter bin,
He can't afford to buy.

Whatever happened to his life,
Son and daughter, darling wife,
Friends, especially best mate Bob,
Hobbies, pastimes, steady job.

No bank account, no home, no car,
Or soft warm feather bed,
No roof to keep the rain away,
No hat upon his head.

His pension cheque does not go far,
Donates it to the local bar.

Sometimes he dines at 'Meals on Wheels,'
Depending on how well he feels.

His shabby looks and ragged clothes
Make people turn away.
Children ask,"Mum, who's that man?"
"He's just a tramp", she'll say.
Life is tough for poor old Jim,
There's not much love for tramps like him.
A friendly chat, a caring smile,
Would make his life much more worthwhile.

But caring people number few,
And most don't spare a thought.
This worn-out soul upon the bench,
Once for his country fought.

Proud and brave and seventeen
He fought against a foe unseen,
Alongside mates and not alone,
But still a boy, so far from home.

Gunfire rang from out the trees,
But brave men stood their ground,
Advancing and returning fire
Despite that fearful sound.

All around him heroes fell,
Boys, now men, alone in hell.
No time to think of friends and lovers,
All these men were now Jim's brothers.

Finally the fighting ceased,

The war was won and lost.
The allied ships then headed home,
The sick and dead the cost.

A hero's welcome on the docks,
A pretty girl with golden locks,
A cheering crowd, a big brass band,
The champions of all the land.

In uniform, with head held high,
A medal on his chest,
Jim's greeted by his hometown friends,
They cheer loudly, "He's the best!"

But now his life is in the park,
Birds still sing, and dogs still bark,
Lovers stroll, and children play,
But a vagrant's life is not so gay.

Today old Jim is "just a tramp,"
A champion no more.
He never sees a uniform,
Except that of the law.

The only token of his past
The medal on his chest,
Reminding him of days gone by,
When he was called "the best."

John Hansen is a freelance writer of short fiction and poetry living in Queensland, Australia. He is a strong advocate for the environment, human rights, equality, and fair distribution of wealth. His work can be found on HubPages among other places.

Mairi Neil

Melbourne Central

The woollen scarf tied as fashion dictates,
as the university student waves
the radical newspaper aloft
and denounces government indifference
bold black print matches strident voice
the queues for takeaway lengthen
business suits sail past,
high heels click-clack
shoppers shuffle with laden bags
people avert their gaze, focus
on smartphone seclusion
the homeward commute seeks
train and tram timetables
they have somewhere to be...
From the shadows movement
a nondescript bundle murmurs
cardboard begging sign sags
and polystyrene cup stands empty

Mairi Neil is an Australian writer with a strong belief in social justice. She founded and co-ordinated for 21 years the community writers' group Mordialloc Writers. She loves writing poetry, short stories and memoir and still blogs at Up the Creek With a Pen believing in the power of words, and sharing our stories and experiences helps build empathetic communities.

About the Editor

James P. Wagner (Ishwa) is an editor, publisher, award-winning fiction writer, essayist, historian, actor, comedian, performance poet, and alum twice over (BA & MALS) of Dowling College. He is the publisher for Local Gems Poetry Press and the Senior Founder and President of the Bards Initiative. He is also the founder and Grand Laureate of Bards Against Hunger, a series of poetry readings and anthologies dedicated to gathering food for local pantries that operates in over a dozen states. His most recent individual collection of poetry is *Everyday Alchemy*. He was the Long Island, NY National Beat Poet Laureate from 2017-2019. He was the Walt Whitman Bicentennial Convention Chairman and has taught poetry workshops at the Walt Whitman Birthplace State Historic Site. James has edited over 100 poetry anthologies and hosted book launch events up and down the East Coast. He was named the National Beat Poet Laureate of the United States from 2020-2021. He is the owner/operator of The Dog-Eared Bard's Book Shop in East Northport, New York.

Made in the USA
Middletown, DE
29 October 2023

41519268R00225